THE 10 GREATEST TEAMS
IN THE BIBLE

THE 10 GREATEST TEAMS IN THE BIBLE

CURTIS MOSLEY

XULON PRESS

Xulon Press
2301 Lucien Way #415
Maitland, FL 32751
407.339.4217
www.xulonpress.com

Unless otherwise indicated, Scripture quotations taken from the New King James Version (NKJV). Copyright © 1982 by Thomas Nelson, Inc. Used by permission. All rights reserved.

Printed in the United States of America.

Paperback ISBN-13: 978-1-6628-0010-8
eBook ISBN-13: 978-1-6628-0011-5

FOREWORD
by PAT WILLIAMS

Author of over 100 books; National Basketball Association Hall-of-Famer; and co-founder of the NBA's Orlando Magic.

Having spent my entire adult life in the study of teamwork and leadership, I view very little material as original or creative. But when an innovative and thought-provoking book like "THE TEN GREATEST TEAMS IN THE BIBLE" appears, I jump in with fresh enthusiasm.

This book illuminates the genius of ten triumphant teams with unique insight and remarkable wisdom, yet in a very readable and entertaining fashion.

The principles, techniques, and characteristics explored apply to your church, athletic team, and business organization.

The golden treasures herein, mined from both the Old and New Testaments, will transform your team into the champion of your dreams.

Additionally, the lively and fun group activities at the end of each chapter will spark discussions that will uncover buried strengths and talents in your team members.

About the Author
CURTIS MOSLEY

Curtis Mosley has taught at LeTourneau University, the University of Phoenix, and Belhaven University. He has operated a successful business for over 26 years.

Among his academic credentials are:
B.A. History, Tulane University.
M.A. Human Resources Management, Pepperdine University.
M.A. Christian Studies, Grand Canyon University.

He is the author of six books and over 60 songs.

His other books are:

RainCatcher: Help from Above for Entrepreneurs
Verses for Nurses
True Blue Lines: God's Laws for Law Enforcement Officers
The Nitty Gritty of Teaching Adult Sunday School
Types of Christ at www.TypesOfChrist.com (Free online)

He has served in many team-building and leadership positions in athletics, church, and business organizations.

Table of Contents

THE BIBLICAL BASIS FOR TEAMS

I f the task is too great for one person, a team is required. Here are six basic reasons for forming teams:

  a. **To prevent burnout**. Stress and emotional burnout are real threats.
  b. **Protection**. Nature teaches that there is safety in numbers. Lions live in prides. Birds fly in flocks.
  c. **Accountability**. Teams foster visibility and positive peer pressure.
  d. **Christian Unity**. Unity is a powerful force. "For where two or three are gathered together in My name, I am there in the midst of them" (Jesus, in Matthew 18:20, NKJV). God blesses brothers living in unity. (Psalm 133)
  e. **Testimony**. A team, working in unity, is an impressive sight: "Awesome as an army with banners!" (Song of Solomon 6:4, NKJV).

I. To accomplish great things without burnout.

(Exodus 18:13-27, ERV)
The next day, Moses had the special job of judging the people. There were so many people that they had to stand before him all day.

Jethro saw Moses judging the people. He asked, "Why are you doing this? Why are you the only judge? And why do people come to you all day?"

Then Moses said to his father-in-law, "The people come to me and ask me to ask for God's decision for their problem. If people have an argument, they come to me, and I decide which person is right. In this way I teach the people God's laws and teachings."

But Moses' father-in-law said to him, "This isn't the right way to do this. It is too much work for you to do alone. You cannot do this job by yourself. It wears you out. And it makes the people tired too. Now, listen to me. Let me give you some advice. And I pray God will be with you. You should continue listening to the problems of the people. And you should continue to speak to God about these things. You should explain God's laws and teachings to the people. Warn them not to break the laws. Tell them the right way to live and what they should do. 21 But you should also choose some of the people to be judges and leaders.

"Choose good men you can trust—men who respect God. Choose men who will not change their decisions for money. Make these men rulers over the people. There should be rulers over 1000 people, 100 people, 50 people, and even over ten people. ²² Let these rulers judge the people. If there is a very important case, then they can come to you and let you decide what to do. But they can decide the other cases themselves. In this way these men will share your work with you, and it will be easier for you to lead the people. If you do this as God directs you, then you will be able to do your job without tiring yourself out. And the people can still have all their problems solved before they return home."

So Moses did what Jethro told him. Moses chose good men from among the Israelites. He made them leaders over the people. There were rulers over 1000 people, 100 people, 50 people, and ten people. ²⁶ These rulers were judges for the people. The people could always bring their arguments to these rulers, and Moses had to decide only the most important cases.

Bear one another's burdens, and so fulfill the law of Christ. (Paul, in Galatians 6:2)

Let each of you look out not only for his own interests, but also for the interests *of others*. (Paul, in Philippians 2:4 NKJV)

Rejoice with them that do rejoice, and weep with them that weep.

Paul, in Romans 12:15
A joy shared is *twice the joy*, but a burden shared is *half the burden.*

II. Protection

King Solomon, in Ecclesiastes 4:9-12, NKJV
Two are better than one, because they have a good reward for their labor.
For if they fall, one will lift up his companion. But woe to him who is alone when he falls,
For he has no one to help him up. Again, if two lie down together, they will keep warm;
But how can one be warm alone? **Though one may be overpowered by another, two can withstand him. And a threefold cord is not quickly broken.**

Proverbs 11:14 (KJV): Where no counsel is, the people fall: but in the multitude of counselors there is safety.

Proverbs 14:28 (KJV): In a multitude of people is a king's honor, but in the lack of people is the downfall of the prince.

Hebrews 10:25, (NKJV): "And let us consider one another in order to stir up love and good works, not forsaking the assembling of ourselves together, as *is* the manner of some, but exhorting one another."

III. Accountability

Acts 11:30, ERV. They gathered the money and gave it to Barnabas and Saul, who took it to the elders in Judea.

Psalms 141:5, ERV. If good people correct me, I will consider it a good thing.

If they criticize me, I will accept it like a warm welcome.

Proverbs 27:5-6.
Open rebuke is better than secret love. Faithful are the wounds of a friend.

IV. Achieve through the power of Unity

Genesis 11: 1-6, ERV
There was a time when the whole world spoke one language. Everyone used the same words. Then people began to move from the East. They found a plain in the land of Babylonia and stayed there to live. ³ Then they said to each other, "Let's make some bricks of clay and bake them in the fire." Then they used these bricks as stones, and they used tar as mortar.

Then the people said, "Let's build ourselves a city and a tower that will reach to the sky. Then we will be famous. This will keep us together so that we will not be scattered all over the earth."

Then the LORD came down to see the city and the tower. The LORD said, "These people all speak the same language. And I see that they are joined together to do this work. This is only the beginning of what they can do. Soon they will be able to do anything they want.

Psalms 133
Behold, how good and how pleasant it is for brethren to dwell together in unity!

It is like the precious ointment upon the head, that ran down upon the beard, even Aaron's beard: that went down to the skirts of his garments;

As the dew of Hermon, and as the dew that descended upon the mountains of Zion: for there **the Lord commanded the blessing**, even life for evermore.

Philippians 2:2-4
Fulfil you my joy, that you be likeminded, having the same love, being of **one accord** (agreement), of one mind. Let nothing be done through strife or vainglory; but in lowliness of mind let each esteem other better than themselves. Look not every man on his own things, but every man also on the things of others.

V. Testimony

Jesus, in John 13:35.
By this shall all men know that you are my disciples, if you have love one to another.

1 Chronicles 12:33.
Of Zebulun, such as went forth to battle, **expert** in war, with all instruments of war, fifty thousand, **which could keep rank**: they were not of double heart.

1 Chronicles 12:38.
All these men of war, that could keep rank, came with a perfect heart.

CHAPTER 1

NOAH AND FAMILY

A Study in Sanctification

O nly nine generations after Adam, the human race had descended into depravity. But God still had a faithful man: Noah. "But Noah was a pleasure to the Lord. Here is the story of Noah. He was the only truly righteous man living on the earth at that time." (Genesis 6:8-10).

The name Noah means "Relief." His parents had named him this because they wanted him to bring "relief from the hard work of farming this ground which God has cursed" (Genesis 5:29, KJV).

God's heart was broken because of the sinfulness on the earth; so He planned to destroy every living thing. Then the Lord said "My Spirit must not forever be disgraced in man, wholly evil as he is" (Genesis 6:3, TLB). "And, behold, I, *even I*, do bring a flood of waters upon the earth, to destroy all flesh, wherein is the breath of life, from under heaven; and everything that is in the earth shall die" (Genesis 6:17, KJV).

When God is outraged, he personally carries out the punishment. He doesn't send an angel.

However, God wanted to protect this one righteous man and his family. So, He commanded Noah to construct a great ship. He also told Noah to bring every kind of animal on board as well as plenty of food. Noah and his family followed God's instructions specifically.

After completion of the ark, God spoke to Noah, "Go into the boat with all your family, for among all the people of the earth, I consider you alone to be righteous. Bring in the animals, too – a pair of each, except those kinds I have chosen for eating and for sacrifice: take seven pairs of each of them, and seven pairs of every kind of bird. Thus, there will be every kind of life reproducing again after the flood has ended. One week from today I will begin forty days and nights of rain; and all the animals and birds and reptiles I have made will die. So Noah did everything the Lord commanded him" (Genesis 7:1-5, TLB).

One week later, torrential rain began and springs of water burst forth. This continued until the earth was completely flooded. "But Noah had gone into the boat that very day with his wife and his sons, Shem, Ham, and Japheth, and their wives" (Genesis 7:13, TLB).

All air-breathing life perished.

150 days after the rain began, the ark came to rest upon a mountain top. Months later, Noah sent out a dove which returned with an olive branch in its beak, proof that the flood had subsided greatly.

The second time Noah released the dove, it did not return. A month later, Noah opened the door of the ark and two months later, the earth was dry again.

Then God told Noah to send the animals out to resume normal life, reproducing and repopulating their species. Noah and his family also disembarked.

Noah Worships God (Genesis 8:20-22)

Upon disembarking, Noah built and altar and sacrificed to God. "And the Lord smelled a sweet savor; and the Lord said in his heart, I will not again curse the ground any more for man's sake" (Genesis 8:21, KJV). Noah had fulfilled the hope of his parents!

God Promises Mercy

God also decreed never again to destroy the earth with a flood and He decided to preserve seasons, schedules, and harvests on the earth. "While the earth remains, seedtime and harvest, and cold and heat, and summer and winter, and day and night shall not cease" (Genesis 8:22, KJV). God confirmed this promise with a rainbow.

God Starts Over (Genesis 9)

There is a great similarity between God's blessings on Adam and Noah. He gave both of them dominion over the earth. Note that Adam and Ever were sinless at the time and that Noah was righteous. God begins with righteousness.

God began with Adam and Eve	GOD started over with Noah and his family
In Genesis 1:28, ERV. God blessed them and said to them, "Have many children. Fill the earth and take control of it. Rule over the fish in the sea and the birds in the air. Rule over every living thing that moves on the earth."	**In Genesis 9:1, ERV.** God blessed Noah and his sons and said to them, "Have many children. Fill the earth with your people."
Genesis 1:29, ERV. God said, "I am giving you all the grain bearing plants and all the fruit trees. These trees make fruit with seeds in it. This grain and fruit will be your food."	**Genesis 9:3, ERV.** In the past, I gave you the green plants to eat. Now every animal will also be food for you. I give you everything on earth— it is yours.

God was starting fresh, beginning with our righteous ancestor, Noah. Without him, God would have destroyed the entire human race. He and his family provided the bridge between extinction and survival. We are all related to Noah and owe him a debt of gratitude. Through Noah, God preserved mankind based on the righteousness of just one man, foreshadowing the salvation made available to all men through Christ.

"The names of Noah's three sons were Shem, Ham, and Japheth. … *From these three sons of Noah came all the nations of the earth.*" (Genesis 9:18-19, TLB)

NOAH and FAMILY:
A Study in Sanctification

QUESTIONS TO CONSIDER

1) **God told Noah to do something that had never been done before to deal with an event that had never occurred before.**
   a) Since there had never been a worldwide flood, do you think Noah doubted the need for an ark?
   b) It took Noah 100 years to build the ark. Do you think that Noah wanted to return to farming before he finished the ark?

2) **In 2 Peter 2:5, the New Testament calls Noah "a preacher of righteousness" But other than his own family, nobody entered the ark. He was a preacher without any converts. How do you think Noah felt about the apathy of everyone around him?**
   a) Is leadership ever found in the crowds?
   b) Are you willing to be mocked while you complete your project?
   c) Do you think you will have an opportunity to drop out inconspicuously?

3) What made Noah persevere?
   a) How did his relationship with God affect his determination and confidence?
   b) To what degree did his family affect his actions?

4) Were the others in Noah's day given the opportunity to board the ark?
   a) Why didn't they believe Noah?
   b) How do you think the mockers reacted when the flood came?

5) What is peer pressure? Did it influence people in Noah's day? How so?
   a) How devastating can peer pressure be?
   b) When is the last time you witnessed it first-hand?
   c) What age groups does peer pressure affect?
   d) Is there such a thing as "positive peer pressure?"
   e) If so, where would you find supportive peers?
   f) How would people with positive attitudes support you?
   g) Do people befriend others who are like them?

6) Notice that Noah built the ark, but God closed the door behind him: "Then the Lord God closed the door and shut them in." In the New Testament, Paul wrote, "For we are laborers together with God" (1 Corinthians 3:9, KJV).
   a) Are we working with God?
   b) Are we working for God?
   c) Is God working in us?

d) Is God working through us?

e) Which is better: doing something for God or God doing something through you?

NOAH and FAMILY:
A Study in Sanctification

GROUP DISCUSSION / ACTIVITIES

Discussion: Alone Again Naturally

Have you ever had to carry out a decision that other people did not like?

How did you maintain your focus and commitment?

When it was over, did those who "missed the boat" wish they had helped?

Objective: To warn team members and leaders about negative peer pressure.

Small Group Discussion: Storms Ahead?

Forecast ten pitfalls that should be avoided.

Identify preventive measures to prevent failure. Classify these responses into:

- Spiritual
- Emotional

- Physical
- Financial
- Time Management
- Personal
- Professional
- Technical Problems
- Other

Objective:

- To look ahead for any hazards.
- To avoid pitfalls.

Smooth Sailing Ahead? Do teams sometimes fail to prepare for success?

In small groups, forecast the best-case scenario: maximum success.

It is easy for God to bless you. "Thus says the LORD, Make this valley full of ditches. For thus says the LORD, "You shall not see wind, neither shall you see rain; yet that valley shall be filled with water, that you may drink." (2 KINGS 3:16-18).

Oftentimes, organizations experience much greater success than they expected.

Are you prepared for success? Is success more hazardous than failure? How so?

Identify the steps to handle the coming success.

Classify these steps into:

- **Spiritual**: Do I have the time to keep this project in my daily prayers?
- **Emotional**: Will I remember that God gives me the strength? "I can do all things through Christ which strengthens me." (Philippians 4:13).
- **Physical**: Will I stay fit?
- **Financial**: Will I remember to honor God with first fruits?
- **Time Management**: Will I manage my time wisely?
- **Personal**: Will I maintain my relationship with loved ones?
- **Professional**: Will I keep up with my professional education? The more you know, the more you grow.
- **Technology**: Will I take advantage of modern technology?
- **Other**: Will I continue to look for ways to improve?

Objective:

- To expect and prepare for success.

Team Discussion: Close Quarters

Noah and his family were on the ark for one year without anyone else to talk to.

- Do you think they got tired of one another?
- If so, how did they keep things friendly?
- Are you able to work with the same people month after month?

Objective: To consider that team members will be seeing a lot of each other.

A healthy team culture is needed to stand the test of time.

Discussion: What for?

The future of the whole world rested on Noah's success.

What depends on your work?

Create a list and discuss five things that depend on you.

Objective: To define specific responsibilities.

Discussion: Trading Places

After Noah completed the ark, he and his family were skilled carpenters.

Some skills you learn during a project are useful for the rest of your life.

Some skills are never used again.

What character development occurs during a major project?

What did God teach Noah that he could use for the rest of his life?

Objective:

- To let them know that some experiences, even though they are absolutely necessary for survival, are only for a season.
- To inform that some work is its own reward.
- To remind that work ethics, such as diligence and high quality, transfer to other different types of work.
- To recognize that new projects require new skill sets.

OBEDIENCE = WISDOM.
10 STEPS to OBEDIENCE

1. Recognize that obedience may be a matter of life and death.
2. Identify the consequences of disobeying God.
3. Ask God for wisdom about which steps to take. "If you need wisdom, ask our generous God, and he will give it to you." (James 1:5). Lacking wisdom is much more detrimental than lacking material.
4. Ask God for energy to do the job. "Strengthen me, I pray" (Judges 16:28, KJV).
5. Disregard opinions, even those of family members, that conflict with God's command and way of doing business.

Although there are four possible responses, only one works.

YOUR WILL. YOUR WAY. = FAILURE	YOUR WILL GOD's WAY. = FAILURE
GOD's WILL. YOUR WAY. = FAILURE	**GOD's WILL.** **GOD's WAY.** **= SUCCESS.**

6. Recognize that obedience is what you would do it you had all the facts. Being planted and being buried look the same.

7. If you do God's will, God's way, you can't lose: "This foolish plan of God is wiser than the wisest of human plans, and God's weakness is stronger than the greatest of human strength (1 Corinthians 1:25).

8. Break the job into small steps. Do one thing at a time. Do the most important task first. Don't get tired. "And let us not get tired of doing what is right, for after a while we will reap a harvest of blessing if we don't get discouraged and give up." (Galatians 6:9).

9. Remember that work is fun. "There is nothing better for men than that they should be happy in their work" (Solomon, in Ecclesiastes 3:22, TLB)

10. Do the small things to the best of your ability. They may become a big factor later. Only the best survive.

CHAPTER 2

GIDEON AND HIS SHOCK TROOPS

A Study in the Psychology
of Victory and Defeat

Before Israel had a king, judges ruled Israel. They were both wise in court and formidable on the battlefield. When the ruling judge died, however, Israel always lapsed back into sin. So, God would stir up a nearby nation to make their lives very miserable. When the oppression became unbearable, the Israelites would cry out to God, and he would give them another judge.

One such time, God allowed the Midianites to dominate Israel for seven years. They destroyed crops and stole livestock so that the entire land was plundered and desolate. The Israelites turned to God.

God chose a farmer named Gideon to deliver his people. Gideon was a cunning military leader: but he didn't know it at the time. "The angel of the LORD appeared and said to him, "The LORD is with you, courageous warrior!" Incredulous, Gideon asked the angel why they were being dominated and why no miracles were happening.

The Lord answered, "Go in this your might, and you shall save Israel from the hand of the Midianites: have not I sent you?" (Judges 6:14). God would not have given him a task if he were not able to complete.

But Gideon contended further, "How can I save Israel? My family is the poorest in the whole tribe of Manasseh, and I am the least thought of in the entire family!" Whereupon the Lord said to him, "But I, Jehovah, will be with you! And you shall **quickly** destroy the Midianite hordes!" (Judges 6:15-16, TLB). Here God reveals the key to victory: **His presence**. God's encouragement to Gideon was the same that He would give to Paul centuries later: "But I am with you, that is all you need. My power shows up best in weak people." (2 Corinthians 12:9, TLB).

The Lord's first assignment for Gideon was to destroy the altar of Baal and the wooden idol Asherah, both of which had been built by Gideon's father! God told Gideon to replace Baal's altar with a stone altar to the Lord and to sacrifice an ox on it, using the wooden idol for firewood! "That same night the LORD said to Gideon, "Choose your father's best bull, the one that is seven years old. First, use it to pull down the altar your father built to worship Baal. Also, cut down the Asherah pole beside the altar. Then build the right kind of altar for the LORD your God. Build it on this high ground. Then kill and burn the bull on this altar. Use the wood from the Asherah pole to burn your offering." (Judges 6:25-26, ERV).

The bull was seven years old; born the same year that the Midianites began to afflict the Israelites! He had been raising the bull for the sacrifice to Himself. God knows the end from the beginning (Isaiah 46:10).

That night, Gideon and ten of his servants replaced the altar of Baal with the altar of God. The men of the city awakened the next morning and were shocked to find their idol in rubble. In anger, they set out to find and kill Gideon. When they approached Gideon's father, he wryly questioned them as to why a powerful god would need mere men to punish Gideon. "If Baal is really a god, let him take care of himself and destroy the one who broke apart his altar" (Judges 6:31 TLB). This question stopped the angry men.

This defense of Gideon resulted in a new name for Gideon, "Jerubbaal," meaning "Let Baal take care of himself!" (Judges 6:32). More importantly, Gideon had dethroned Baal and Asherah and restored honor to God. The spiritual priority had been corrected. Next would come the earthly confrontation.

The Midianites and the Amalekites massed to prepare for battle. But God is not concerned by large armies. "But the spirit of the Lord came upon Gideon, and he blew a trumpet." (Judges 6:33-34, KJV). The sound of the trumpet stirred his fellow Israelites and they answered the call.

In fact, too many Israelites answered the call, because God did not want this battle won by a large Israeli army. The purpose of the war was to bring honor to God. "And the Lord said unto Gideon, 'The people that are with you are too many for me to give the Midianites into their hands, lest Israel vaunt themselves against me, saying, 'My own hand has saved me.'" (Judges 7:2, KJV). God had a delicate task ahead of him: crushing 135,000 enemy troops without his people becoming arrogant. So, Gideon sent home all who were fearful. But there were still too many Israelites. He then tested the remaining men by bringing them down to the water to drink. He chose those who remained watchful as they drank: 300 elite warriors.

In God's mind, the battle had already been won. God spoke of it in the past tense. "Arise, get down unto the host; for I *have delivered* it into your hand" (Judges 7:9).

Like most people, Gideon needed encouragement. He was still developing into the leader he was meant to be.

God allowed him to take his servant with him to spy on the enemy camp. Gideon heard two enemy soldiers talking about "*the sword of Gideon*" (Judges 7:14, KJV). When he heard this, Gideon knew that the Midianites were afraid. They were edgy and prone to overreact.

Before returning to his own camp, Gideon worshipped God. And Gideon began to speak in the past tense: "Arise; for the Lord *has delivered* into your hand the host of Midian." (Judges 7:15). Gideon is no longer apprehensive, but sure of victory.

Through psychological warfare, Gideon planned to exploit the Midianites most vulnerable weakness: fear. This fatal weakness was all Gideon needed to defeat the entire army, but his strategy required stealth and shock.

Gideon armed each warrior with a trumpet and a torch. The torch was concealed by a pitcher. The Israelites quietly encircled the enemy camp just as the Midianites' second watch came on. The guards were not quite settled into their routine when Gideon initiated a barrage of sound and light. Three hundred and one flaming torches instantly surrounded the panicked camp. Gideon's men blew their trumpets and shouted, "The sword of the Lord, and of Gideon." Those terrifying words had been used by the Midianite soldier the night before. "The fear of the wicked will come upon him." (Proverbs 10:24, NKJV). In the face of what appeared to be a vastly superior enemy, the stunned and confused Midianites turned upon themselves, killing one another and fleeing for their lives.

Success encouraged Gideon's allies. Following the rout of the Midianite camp, Gideon called on the men of Ephraim to help pursue the fleeing enemy. They overtook them, capturing and killing two princes. But the men of Ephraim felt shunned because Gideon had not used them in the initial battle. With the diplomacy of his father, Gideon addressed them: "'God let you capture Oreb and Zeeb, the generals of the army of Midian! What have I done in comparison with that? Your actions at the end of the battle were more important than ours at the beginning!' So they calmed down." (Judges 8:2-3).

Following the victory, the Israelites tried to make Gideon their ruler. But Gideon wisely replied: "I will not rule over you, neither shall my son rule over you: *the Lord shall rule over you*" (Judges 8: 23, KJV).

The Making of a Leader

How does a farmer, lowly in his own eyes, become the leader of a commando unit? One step at a time. In reviewing the account, Gideon needed encouragement at every stage. When the angel appeared to him, Gideon asked him to stay long enough for him to give him a present, which the angel consumed by fire (Judges 6:21). When God said Gideon would save Israel, Gideon requested a sign: dew upon a fleece of wool, and God gave him this sign (Judges 6:37). Gideon asked for a second sign, dryness upon the fleece and dew all around, which God arranged. (Judges 6:40). When Gideon was fearful to spy on the enemy camp, God let his servant accompany him (Judges 7:11, KJV). After all, God had promised, "*Surely I will be with you* (Judges 6:16, KJV)." Time and again, from start to finish and every step in between, God stayed with Gideon.

Perhaps God chose Gideon *because* he had a humble opinion of himself. And perhaps because Gideon couldn't take any more from the Midianites. Or because it takes a man with weaknesses to detect vulnerabilities. Gideon's early life of trepidation was also one of preparation. "O the depth of the riches both of the wisdom and knowledge of God! How unsearchable are his judgments, and his ways past finding out!" (Romans 11:33).

With God's encouragement, Gideon overcame self-doubt. God transformed his self-image from a field hand to a field general. But God changed the mighty Midianites into a panic-stricken mob. The Lord's presence girded Gideon with strength and confidence, but he completely debilitated the enemy.

Gideon did not alter his strength, his upbringing or his skill. But he did change something more powerful than any of these: he changed his mindset. Once Gideon saw himself as God did, he became the leader he was created to be. "For as he thinks in his heart, so is he" (Proverbs 23:7).

Confidence comes from right standing with God. Proverbs 28:1 tells us that "The godly are bold as lions!" If you fear God, you won't fear man.

There are war heroes, yet unknown, who can be found tending wheat in country fields. There are also small bands of courageous men, who by skill and cunning, outflank vast armies in the night.

GIDEON AND HIS SHOCK TROOPS:

A STUDY IN THE PSYCHOLOGY OF VICTORY AND DEFEAT

QUESTIONS TO CONSIDER

1. **You must win the spiritual battle before you begin the physical battle.**

   Jesus said you must defeat the evil one before taking his place and his goods.

   "Satan must be bound before his demons are cast out,ᴵ just as a strong man must be tied up before his house can be ransacked and his property robbed." (Mark 3:27, TLB). Are there any false gods in your way? Are you depending on your own strength? Are you completely dependent on God for success? "Every good gift and every perfect gift is from above, and comes down from the Father of lights" (James 1:7, KJV)

   What worthless things stand between you and your goal? If there is anything between you and God, God will destroy it. So, you might as well give it up now. In Exodus 20:15, God said, "I will not share your affection with any other god!"

Gideon's first assignment was tearing down the false gods. Your devotion cannot be split. The human mind can only think about one thing at a time. Before you embark on your new journey, you will have to destroy some things from the past.

a. What are the top three time-consuming candidates for elimination?
b. How will life in the future be altered by dropping them?
c. Keep in mind that some people may not like your new priorities. Gideon ran into resistance when he knocked down the old order. Putting God first may ruffle some feathers at first.
d. Is it stressful to be overcommitted?
e. Faith is about focus. Is it better to be a laser beam or a floodlight?
f. What is the difference between tension and stress?

2. **Consider how the angel addressed Gideon:**

   The Lord is with you, *you mighty man of valor.*

   This greeting was quite surprising to Gideon, a farmer by trade. He had never viewed himself as a brave warrior. Yet, God knew that Gideon, deep inside, had an uncommon desire to obey his will.

   a. Is there a parallel between Gideon and yourself?

b. Is there great chivalry, bravery, and valor hidden inside you?

You should never have a low opinion of yourself. **YOU ARE MADE IN THE IMAGE OF GOD!** God's attributes reside in you! courage, creativity, intelligence, personality, and honor! You have God's "DNA" and you know it. "I am fearfully and wonderfully made: marvelous are your works; and that my soul knows right well" (Psalm 139:14, KJV). Deep down, you know that you are a marvelous and brilliant creation of the most skilled Artisan of all: God Himself! Is it any wonder that he brought you here to serve his purpose in this very hour? Yes, God himself has directed you here! Why? To develop, to praise him, to serve him, and to be fruitful. In other words, he brought you here to be like him. You are God's masterpiece.

Next, notice Gideon's instructions: And the Lord looked upon him, and said, _Go in this your might_. The irony of good teams is that they depend on individual performance. Unless each person does her part, the whole team suffers. A team is only as strong as its weakest team member.

This means that each member should be assigned a role for which she is well suited. In other words, do the job that requires your gifts and talents. (Normally, this is the job that you **want** to do). Do not try to force square pegs into round holes. The secret to team success is found in Ephesians 4:16: "from whom the whole body, joined and knit together by what every joint supplies, according to the effective working by which **every part does its share**, causes growth of the body for the edifying of itself in love. If each person does his part, the whole team will succeed.

a. What does it mean to "Go in this your might?"
b. Is God's command God's equipping?
c. Do you have strengths that God has given you to achieve success?
d. Can you list 10 of these and categorize them into physical, mental, emotional, or spiritual characteristics?
e. How did you acquire these abilities? Through experience? By training? By upbringing? By birth?
f. Which gifts do you most **enjoy** using?
g. Are you more likely to do a good job if you enjoy the work?
h. In the past, which gifts have you used successfully at work?
i. Which type work have **other people** complimented you on?

Also note that it was God who sent Gideon: "**have not I sent you?**" God would never have sent Gideon unless he was well able. God is sovereign (in control) of everything, so he would not have brought you here if you were not up to the task.

3. **Notice that God promised to accompany Gideon:** <u>**And the Lord said unto him, Surely I will be with you.**</u>" Do you know that you have Someone who will be right there with you all the time? **Make God the Captain of your team and you will always achieve your goals.** (John 6:21): "Then they were willing to let him in, and immediately the boat was where they were going!" The Lord will take you where you should be.

4. **We Walk by Faith, Not Sight. Gideon was outnumbered.** Perhaps you feel the same way as you survey the task and the time available. But Gideon was undeterred. When he blew the trumpet, his fellow soldiers answered the call. You may find that there are talented people around you who are willing to help. God is able to provide you with the team members you need to accomplish the task at hand. But do not divulge confidential information to untrustworthy associates. "Don't tell your secrets to a gossip unless you want them broadcast to the world" (Proverbs 20:19, TLB). If you're swimming with sharks, don't bleed. The key to victory is to read God's Word and not be distracted by the commotion.

5. Please don't feel alone and isolated as you proceed. If you need help, ask for it. Read the Bible! Remember to pray! "The effectual fervent prayer of a righteous man avails much." (James 5:16)

a. If you need to ask for help, to whom should you go?
b. Should you say **specifically** where the problem is?
c. Are you willing to help a coworker?

6. **Gideon took time to think.** He devised both grand strategy and detailed tactics. A good theory is quite useful! Paying close scrutiny to **details** is the difference between a car running well and one that really purrs. Solomon wrote about, "the **little** foxes, that spoil the vines." (Song of Solomon 2:15). Gideon taught and trained his soldiers thoroughly. Remember, practice does not make perfect: **perfect** practice makes perfect. Although victory comes from the Lord, we should never test the Lord by poor preparation. Preparation is the secret to life.

a. Do you enjoy planning and coordinating?
b. Are you willing to rehearse with your team prior to each presentation?
c. Is any team only as strong as its weakest link?
d. Is a team much stronger than the sum of its individual members?
e. What is synergy?
f. How important is the leader to the success of the team? Why?
g. Are you willing to pray as a group before your assignments?

7. **By the end of story, Gideon had become a courageous leader.**

    a. How was Gideon able to maintain his focus until the end?

    b. How would you explain such a complete change in attitude?

    c. How many people are capable of serving God in dramatic ways?

    d. Do they know their own potential?

    e. What steps are required to achieve your fullest potential?

    f. What is God's role in helping you reach your full potential?

    g. What transformed Gideon from a nobody to a war hero? Was it God's presence? "And the LORD said unto him, Surely I will be with you, and you shall smite the Midianites as one man." (Judges 6:16).

8. **Does God need many people to defeat the enemy?**

    a. He can win a battle whether he has many warriors or only a few! (1 Samuel 14:6, TLB).

    b. The LORD will cause your enemies who rise against you to be defeated before you. They shall come out against you one way and flee before you seven ways. (Deuteronomy 28:7, ESV).

9. **Does God need much time to destroy your enemies?**
   a. And you shall **quickly** destroy the Midianite hordes!
   b. Then they just stood and watched as the whole vast enemy army began rushing around in a panic, shouting and running away (Judges 7:21). "My eyes have seen the downfall of my enemies; my ears have heard the defeat of my wicked opponents" (Psalm 92:11, NLT).

10. **Should we always trust that God is infinitely more powerful than the enemy?**

   a. The Angel touched the meat and bread with his staff, and fire flamed up from the rock and consumed them! (Judges 6:21, TLB). Then Gideon said to the Lord, "Please don't be angry with me, but let me make one more test: this time let the fleece remain dry while the ground around it is wet!" So the Lord did as he asked; that night the fleece stayed dry, but the ground was covered with dew! (Judges 6:39-40, TLB).

11. **Is diplomacy critical in dealing with people?**

   a. But Joash retorted to the whole mob, "Does Baal need your help?" (Judges 6:31, TLB).
   b. But Gideon replied, "God let you capture Oreb and Zeeb, the generals of the army of Midian! What have I done in comparison with

that" Your actions at the end of the battle were more important than ours at the beginning!" So they calmed down. (Judges 6:2-3, TLB). The New Testament teaches us: "Do nothing out of rivalry or vanity; but, in humility, regard each other as better than yourselves — (Philippians 2:3, CJB).

12. Should we expect God to use the enemies' own strengths against them?

    a. Now the Midianites and Amalekites, all the people of the East, were lying in the valley as numerous as locusts; and their camels were without number, as the sand by the seashore in multitude. (Judges 7:12, NKJV)

    b. Then they just stood and watched as the whole vast enemy army began rushing around in a panic, shouting and running away. For in the confusion the Lord caused the enemy troops to begin fighting and killing each other from one end of the camp to the other. (Judges 7:21-22, TLB).

    c. Proverbs 26:27, ESV reads, "Whoever digs a pit will fall into it, and a stone will come back on him who starts it rolling."

16. Is giving encouragement important for both leaders and followers?

a. But I, Jehovah, will be with you! And you shall quickly destroy the Midianite hordes! (Judges 6:16, TLB)

b. When Gideon heard the dream and the interpretation, all he could do was just stand there worshiping God! Then he returned to his men and shouted, "Get up! For the Lord is going to use you to conquer all the vast armies of Midian!" (Judges 7:15, TLB). Once the leader, Gideon, was encouraged, he passed the encouragement on to others.

c. But thanks be to God, who always leads us in victory through Christ. (2 Corinthians 2:14, TLB). With God, you can't lose. So, don't quit!

Gideon and His Shock Troops

A Study in the Psychology of Victory and Defeat

DISCUSSION QUESTIONS AND ACTIVITIES

Getting to know one another and letting others get to know you:

Break up into groups of two.

Have each student interview the other for the purposes of:

    a. Introducing the team member to the others.
    b. Identifying strengths of each team member.

Objective: To identify, clarify, and appreciate the strengths of others.

Role-Playing: "Live on the Air":

- Invite one person play the role of a news reporter who will interview Gideon **after** the battle.
- Another volunteer can play the role of Gideon.

Possible questions may be:

- How did you feel when …the angel appeared, the Midianites panicked, when you knocked down the idol Baal, etc.
- Did you feel equipped when you took over as the leader?
- Would you do it again?
- Was there anything difficult about being the leader?
- How do your fellow countrymen feel about you?
- Is your self-confidence stronger now?
- Do you have stronger faith in God?
- Did you undertake this campaign for God, your countrymen, or for yourself?

(You can also have someone play the role of one of **Gideon's soldiers** and ask how they felt about Gideon's leadership).

Objective: To clarify what achieving success will mean.

Small Group Interaction: "Rank the Traits"

In small groups, prioritize the top 10 personality traits of Gideon from 1 to 10.

Share them with the other groups.

Someone can write them on the board in front of the class.

Ask groups how they ranked traits.

Objective: To identify personality traits that are admired and valued by others.

Small Group Interaction "What is success?"

Define **Gideon's** idea of success in one sentence.

Is your definition of success similar to Gideon's?

Is there a difference between long term success and short-term success?

Share with the team.

Objective: To challenge team members to reconsider their ideas of success.

Small Group Interaction: "Looking Ahead"

Identify one or two things that could have caused Gideon to fail.

How did he avoid them? Share with the class.

Objective: To forecast potential pitfalls ahead.

Small Group interaction: "Lightening Your Load"

Each group compiles a list of things that they plan to give up to have time.

Objective: To brainstorm about the topic of time management to avoid cumulative stress.

Role Playing: "Keep your Eyes on the Prize"

Invite attendees to play the role of Gideon **BEFORE** the angel appeared to him. (Before his successful military campaign). Another "news reporter" can ask him:

- Do you think your country is able to live free from your enemies?
- How powerful are your enemies?

- Do you think they can be defeated?
- Do you think God knows your situation?
- Do you think God will help you?

Then, have the same reporter ask the same student the same questions, but have the student play the role of Gideon **AFTER** his great military victory.

Finally, have each team member speak for two minutes (two minutes for each question) about:

- How they feel right now <u>before</u> completing the upcoming project
- How they will feel when they have completed the project.

The first two minutes could address expectations, anticipated problems, and what they hope to achieve.

The last two minutes, could begin with a phrase like, "Looking back on my time here, I felt that it gave me a sense of _____ and more skill in _____ and _____. I feel _____. My supervisor now views me as _____.

I have no regrets because I put _____ % into my work.

Objective: To create an image of finishing the project and an expectation of satisfaction from a job well done.

CHAPTER 3

David and the Armies of the Living God

A Study in Transformational Leadership

"He raises up the poor out of the dust, and lifts up the beggar from the dunghill, to set them among princes, and to make them inherit the throne of glory."
1 Samuel 2: 8

THE BEGINNING OF DAVID's ARMY

God's favor for David were as great as his disfavor for Saul. Saul knew it was only a matter of time before David assumed the throne. Enraged by jealousy, Saul sought to kill David "because the Lord was with him, and was departed from Saul" (1 Samuel 18:12). David was also extremely popular among the people, the subject of songs and admiration. "All

Israel and Judah loved David, because he went out and came in before them" (1 Samuel 18: 14-16, KJV).

So David fled from the serial predator Saul. But David found that there were others on the run also, fleeing from debt and other bad situations. Like David, they had no place to call home. "And every one that was in distress, and every one that was in debt, and every one that was discontented, gathered themselves unto him; and he became a captain over them: and there were with him about four hundred men" (1 Samuel 22:2, KJV).

How quickly God met David's need for an army! And how wonderfully God met the soldiers' need for a leader! Both were in distress and on the run.

LOYALTY DEVELOPED

David had great compassion for these men and welcomed them. One that came to him was Abiathar, a priest whose father Saul had murdered for helping David. David wanted to honor Abiathar's father for the kindness he had shown. So David gave Abiathar a pledge of loyalty: "Abide with me, fear not: for he that seeks my life seeks your life: but with me you shall be safe" (1 Samuel 22:23, KJV). David was doing much more than merely commenting that he and Abiathar both had Saul as an enemy; he was pledging his own life to protect Abiathar. To threaten Abiathar was to threaten David. David's men were loyal because of his commitment. And he offered the one thing they wanted: a secure place on the team. David expressed how important and valuable they were to him and the soldiers appreciated it dearly.

DAVID's MEN SUDDENLY ESTEEMED

David's men did not come to him as brave, well-trained troops. When first given the opportunity to battle the Philistines, they responded meekly: "Behold, we are afraid here in Judah: how much more then if we come to Keilah against the armies of the Philistines?" (1 Samuel 23:3, KJV). It was stressful enough for them among their own people, and now David wanted them to engage Israel's arch enemy. Upon hearing their response, David turned to God and was reassured of victory. "So David and his men went to Keilah … and smote them with a great slaughter" (1 Samuel 23:5, KJV).

With the victory over the Philistines, David's men acquired a new found sense of self-worth and became heroes to the citizens of Keilah. They had saved a city, established a reputation for fighting, and gained much needed experience.

JONATHAN ENCOURAGED DAVID

Immediately following the victory at Keilah, David's army grew to about 600 men. But Saul saw an opportunity to trap David in Keilah because the city was walled (1 Samuel 23:7, KJV). Hearing of Saul's plans to encircle the city, David asked God for guidance. God told him that it would not be safe to stay in Keilah, so David went into the wilderness.

Proverbs 22:3 warns that "Sensible people will see trouble coming and avoid it, but an unthinking person will walk right into it and regret it later." Jonathan, Saul's own son, came to David in the forest and "strengthened his hand in God" (1 Samuel 23:16, KJV). David thought upon God's strength and appreciated the encouragement and fellowship of his dear friend Jonathan.

DAVID TRUSTED GOD TO JUDGE SAUL

During Saul's next mission against David, he unknowingly walked into the very cave in which David was hiding. It is interesting that David's men did not attribute this advantage simply to good fortune. They credited God for this opportunity. "And the men of David said unto him, Behold the day of which the Lord said unto you, Behold, I will deliver your enemy into your hand ..." (1 Samuel 24:4, KJV). David's soldiers had come to understand that God was responsible for their successes. The army respected David, but they did not worship him.

Despite the urging of his men to kill his adversary, David chose to spare Saul's life because God had earlier anointed Saul. David's response to Saul: "The Lord judge between me and you, and the Lord avenge me of you: but my hand shall not be upon you" (1 Samuel 24:12, KJV).

SAUL IN DAVID's HANDS AGAIN

Once again, Saul set out to kill David, pursuing him into the wilderness of Zith with 3,000 men. But David's spies reported Saul's movements in detail. One night, David asked for a volunteer to go with him into Saul's camp. Abishai came forward. He and David crept through the enemy ranks and found Saul sleeping soundly in a trench. Abishai acknowledged God for this opportunity and asked David to allow him to kill Saul: "God has delivered your enemy into your hand this day: now therefore let me smite him ..." (1 Samuel 26:8). But David denied Abishai his request and explained that God would deal with Saul: "The Lord shall smite him; or his day shall come to die; or he shall descend into battle, and perish" (1 Samuel 26: 9-10, KJV).

As Saul slept, David took his spear and canteen. He then slipped away to a safe place and called to his adversaries to let them know that he could have killed Saul. David undertook this treacherous raid into the enemy camp simply to declare his innocence regarding Saul.

It interesting to note that David subsequently appointed Abishai as a commander (2 Samuel 18:2, KJV). David selected commanders based on demonstrated bravery.

GOD INTERVENED ON DAVID's BEHALF

In a later encounter, when Saul had David surrounded, a messenger arrived to tell Saul that the

Philistines had invaded Israel. He had to abandon his pursuit of David and return home. God used one of Israel's enemies to preserve David's life.

DAVID REMOVED HIMSELF FROM SAUL's REACH

To completely remove himself from Saul's reach, David left Israel to live in a neighboring country. There the ruling king gave him a town called Ziklag.

In Ziklag, things went well for David until one day when he and his men were away. The Amalekites set fire to Ziklag, and carried away the women and children and their belongings. Distraught and grief-stricken, the soldiers began to clamor about stoning David. The soldiers were irrational and he himself was in anguish about the loss of his own family. Here David faced a defining moment; his decision would determine the success or failure of his army as well as his own future.

Other than the priest, David was the only one who maintained his senses. David could have collapsed emotionally, argued with his troops, and allowed the army to descend into anarchy – but he didn't. With no one offering a kind word, David "encouraged himself in the Lord" (1 Samuel 30:6, KJV). Sometimes we have to cheer ourselves to victory based on God's promise to never forsake us. And David knew that God's presence means God's triumph.

God told David to pursue the Amalekites and assured him that he would recover both loved ones and property. So David and his men set out in hot pursuit. It was twilight when David and his army found the Amalekites. The Israelites struck them as they were celebrating and slaughtered them all night and until sundown the next day.

DAVID VALUED ALL SOLDIERS EQUALLY

In the course of chasing the Amalekites, two hundred of David's men had grown too tired to continue and had remained at the brook of Besor. David and the remaining 400 warriors went on to defeat the Amalekites.

Because of this, dissension arose in the ranks as some of the men who had fought against the Amalekites objected to sharing the spoils with the 200 soldiers who had stayed behind. "Then said David, You shall not do so, my brethren, with that which the Lord has given us, who has preserved us, and delivered the company that came against us into our hand. For who will hearken unto you in this matter? But as his part is that goes down to the battle, so shall his part be that tarries by the stuff: *they shall part alike*" (1 Samuel 30:23, 34, KJV). David first declared that God had given them the victory, pointing out that no one had any reason for pride. David's pronouncement that all 600 soldiers would receive the same share of the spoils showed that David valued each soldier's contribution equally. Furthermore, David institutionalized this policy of equal reward for the frontline troops and those in the rear guard. "And it was so from that day forward, that he made it a statute and an ordinance for Israel unto this day" (1 Samuel 30:24, KJV). This prevented some from creating an "upper class" based on the job they performed.

DAVID's NEMESIS MET HIS BITTER END

While David was consolidating power, Saul met his bitter end. The Philistines defeated the Israelites in battle and Saul committed suicide to avoid capture.

THE TRIBE OF JUDAH ANNOINTED DAVID KING

"And the men of Judah came, and there they anointed David king over the house of Judah" (2 Samuel 2:4, KJV). David's first act as the King of Judah was to recognize some valiant men who had traveled all night to recover Saul's body and give him a proper burial. "Blessed are you of the Lord, that you have showed this kindness unto your lord, even unto Saul, and have buried him. And now the Lord show kindness and truth unto you: and I also will requite you this kindness, because ye have done this thing" (2 Samuel 2: 5, 6, KJV). David's integrity was again evident in repaying these brave men. David always made it a point to honor and reward those who served God.

DAVID ALSO FOUGHT SAUL's SON

Just after David assumed the throne, Saul's son Ishbosheth, and his general Abner confronted

David. David's battle-hardened troops killed 360 Israelites, losing only 20 men themselves (2 Samuel 2: 30, 31, KJV).

Although this turned into a protracted struggle, the Lord continued to prosper David. "Now there was long war between the house of Saul and the house of David: but David grew stronger and stronger" (2 Samuel 3:1, KJV).

DAVID CROWNED KING OF THE ENTIRE NATION

Eventually, David's general, Joab, killed his enemy counterpart Abner. Ishbosheth himself was then assassinated and David was officially crowned King over all Israel. King David immediately seized the opportunity to take his combined army to battle. He led his troops against the stronghold of Jerusalem. David was especially aroused about this battle because the Jebusites had insulted his army, calling them "the blind and the lame" (2 Samuel 5:6, KJV). David's men entered through the water tunnel and conquered the city, establishing Jerusalem as "The City of David." "So David became greater and greater, for the Lord God of heaven was with him" (2 Samuel 5:10 TLB).

AN OLD ENEMY

The Philistines marshaled their troops in the valley of Rephaim. As usual, David "inquired of the Lord" (2 Samuel 5:19, KJV). The Lord instructed

David to go to battle and he defeated the Philistines. Immediately after the victory, the Israelites honored God by burning the idols which the Philistines had discarded on the battlefield.

But the Philistines regrouped to attack again. David, *even though he had just defeated the Philistines*, did not take the Philistines lightly. Once more, he asked God for guidance. And God gave David instructions on where and when to attack. "And David did so, as the Lord had commanded him; and smote the Philistines from Geba until you come to Gazer" (2 Samuel 5:25, KJV). *David always "inquired of the Lord" before every battle, large or small.*

DAVID'S ARMY DOMINATED THE REGION and HONORED GOD AFTER EVERY VICTORY

The army, which had begun as a small group of outcasts, reeled off victory after victory as Israel increased its domination of the region. The Israelites defeated the Philistines, the Moabites, the cities of Zobah, and the Syrians. "And the Lord preserved David whithersoever he went" (2 Samuel 8:6, KJV). David honored God by dedicating captured treasures to him. "King David dedicated these articles to the LORD, as he had done with the silver and gold from all the nations he had subdued:" (2 Samuel 8:11, NIV).

DAVID's ARMY OCCUPIED CONQUERED REGIONS

"And then placed garrisons throughout Edom, so that the entire nation was forced to pay tribute to Israel—another example of the way the Lord made him victorious wherever he went." (2 Samuel 8:14, TLB). Following victories, Israel's army extracted commercial gain from these lands.

A NEW AMMONITE KING INSULTED DAVID

The Ammonite prince Hanun assumed the throne upon the death of his father. David kindly sent emissaries to Hanun to show respect for his deceased father. However, the new king publicly humiliated David's men and sent them away. Knowing that David would react to the abuse of his men, the Ammonites hired Syrian mercenaries to join with them in war against Israel. The Israelites, under the command of Joab and his brother Abishai, went to battle against the combined Syrian and Ammonite forces. Joab's men fought against the Syrians while Abishai battled the Ammonites. Both the Ammonites and Syrians fled, but the Syrians reinforced and reassembled. David then took charge and "gathered all Israel together" (2 Samuel 10: 17, KJV). Under David's battlefield command, the army killed over 40,000 enemy warriors, including 700 charioteers (2 Samuel 10:18, KJV).

DAVID RECEIVED THE GLORY FOR THE FALL OF RABBAH

Joab later led a force that besieged the Ammonite city of Rabbah. Joab realized that the city was falling and wanted David to gain the honor for the victory. So Joab sent word to David to deliver the final blow. "Now therefore gather the rest of the people together, and encamp against the city, and take it: lest I take the city, and it be called after my name" (2 Samuel 12:28, KJV). David's reputation continued to grow.

DAVID's OWN SON ABSALOM CONSPIRED AGAINST HIM

The most handsome man in Israel was David's son Absalom: "from the sole of his foot even to the crown of his head there was no blemish in him." (2 Samuel 14:25, KJV) But Absalom was also a polished manipulator of people. For 40 years, he gradually and carefully gained support among the populace, taking sides in legal issues and gaining favor among the people. He eventually gained such strength that David had to flee for his life. During this time of emotional stress and physical danger, David wrote the powerful Third Psalm:

"O Lord, so many are against me. So many seek to harm me. I have so many enemies. So many say that God will never help me. But Lord, you are my shield, my glory, and my only hope. You alone can lift my head, now bowed in shame.

I cried to the Lord, and he heard me from his Temple in Jerusalem. Then I lay down and slept in peace and woke up safely, for the Lord was watching over me. And now, although ten thousand enemies surround me on every side, I am not afraid. I will cry to him, 'Arise, O Lord! Save me, O my God!' And he will slap them in the face, insulting them and breaking off their teeth. For salvation comes from God. What joys he gives to all his people" (Psalm 3 TLB).

SOME REMAINED LOYAL TO DAVID

A formidable group of David's servants remained loyal to him. One especially dedicated man was Ittaithe, the Gittite, who, with his 600 men, joined David. David told him to return to Jerusalem, but Ittaithe declared his loyalty: "Surely in what place my lord the king shall be, whether in death or life, even there also will your servant be" (2 Samuel 15:21, KJV). Here was a man who would follow David even to the death.

The priests held the ark of the covenant of God as David and his troops left Jerusalem. Heartbroken, David told them to take the ark back to the city: "Carry back the ark of God into the city: if I shall find favor in the eyes of the Lord, he will bring me again, and show me both it, and his habitation" (2 Samuel 15:25, KJV). Although downcast, David knew that, if it was God's will, he would be restored to the throne.

DAVID DIRECTED THE PRIESTS TO KEEP HIM INFORMED

David's utilized spies and informants to know what his enemy was doing. He used Zadok the priest in such a manner. "Then the king told Zadok, 'Look, here is my plan. Return quietly to the city with your son Ahimaaz and Abiathar's son Jonathan. I will stop at the ford of the Jordan River and wait there for a message from you. Let me know what happens in Jerusalem before I disappear into the wilderness'" (2 Samuel 15: 27, 28 TLB).

DAVID's CHIEF COUNSELOR DEFECTED TO ABSALOM

Absalom secured the services of David's chief advisor, Ahithophel. To counter the loss of such a great asset, David did two things. First, he asked God to discredit his advice to Absalom or "turn the counsel of Ahithophel into foolishness" (2 Samuel 15:31, KJV). Secondly, he sent a trusted friend named Hushai to Absalom to feign the role of counselor, but in reality, to thwart Ahithophel's advice. Additionally, David directed Hushai to pass on intelligence information to the priests, who would keep David informed. Subsequently, Absalom consulted with both the defector Ahithophel and with Hushai.

Ahithophel asked for an expeditionary force of 12,000 elite men to locate and kill David. But Hushai convinced Absalom that such a force would not find the intrepid David. Hushai used David's reputation for valor to draw Absalom into conflict with David: "For all Israel knows that your father is a mighty man, and they which be with him are valiant men" (2 Samuel 17:10, KJV). By this time, David's and his men had attained an intimidating reputation which affected the strategy of their enemies.

It is noteworthy that Ahithophel, who had betrayed David, hanged himself in disgrace following Absalom's refusal to follow his advice (2 Samuel 17:23, KJV).

DAVID's ARMY REFUSED TO ALLOW DAVID TO RISK HIS LIFE IN THE BATTLE AGAINST ABSALOM

David organized his forces equally under Joab, Abishai, and Ittai the Gittite. He then announced that he would personally lead the army. But his men would not let him go in harm's way. "You are worth ten thousand of us, and it is better that you stay here in the city and send us help if we need it" (2 Samuel 18:3, KJV). His men were more concerned for David's life than for their own!

ABSALOM DEFEATED

In the wilderness of Ephraim, David's troops pushed back Absalom's forces on a day that saw 20,000 men die. Contrary to David's orders, Joab killed David's rebellious son Absalom, whose followers then disbursed.

DAVID WAS GRACIOUS IN VICTORY

"So the king went out and sat at the city gates, and … everyone went to him" (2 Samuel 19: 8-10 TLB). David sent Zadok and Abiathar to the elders of Judah to inquire about reinstating him as king. He also appointed Amasa, his nephew, to take Joab's place as commander of the army.

"So the king started back to Jerusalem. And when he arrived at the Jordan River, it seemed as if everyone in Judah had come to Gilgal to meet him and escort him across the river!" (2 Samuel 19:15 TLB).

Shime-i, who had cursed David severely when he evacuated Jerusalem, fell down before the king and pleaded for mercy. One of David's commanders, Abishai, recommended death, but David replied: "This is not a day for execution but for celebration! I am once more king of Israel! Then, turning to Sheme-i, he vowed, 'your life is spared'" (2 Samuel 19:22, 23 TLB).

David had a strong desire to reward Barzillai, who had provided his army with food while in hiding from Absalom. He offered him a home in Jerusalem, but Barzillai declined. However, Barzillai allowed his son Chimham to go with David. "Good," the king agreed. "Chimham shall go with me, and I will do for him whatever I would have done for you" (2 Samuel 19: 37 TLB). As always, David rewarded those who had helped him. This is a godly trait because Hebrews 11:6 teaches that God is a rewarder.

DAVID FACED YET ANOTHER CALAMITY

In the midst of all the celebration about David regaining the throne of Israel, a dispute arose. Because only the tribes of Judah and Benjamin had been given the honor of ferrying David across the Jordan River, the others had become jealous. In the end, all the tribes, except for Judah and Benjamin, abandoned David to follow a short-tempered trouble causer named Sheba.

DAVID SENT AN EXPEDITION AGAINST SHEBA

David sent Abishai and Joab, along with an elite group of soldiers, to hunt down Sheba. During this expedition, Joab killed David's nephew, Amasa, the new commander. Following the assassination, Joab continued to track Sheba and located him in the city of Abel. The citizens agreed to kill Sheba to avert an attack by Joab.

DAVID NEARLY LOST HIS LIFE

"Once when the Philistines were at war with Israel, and David and his men were in the thick of the battle, David became weak and exhausted. Ishbi-benob, a giant...closed in on David and was about to kill him. But Abishai the son of Zeruiah intervened, killing the Philistine. After that, David's men declared, 'You are not going out to battle again! Why should we risk snuffing out the light of Israel?'" (2 Samuel 21:

15-17 TLB). David's men nearly witnessed a loss too great to bear. Despite their need for his leadership in battle, they knew that he was too valuable to risk. In referring to David as "the light of Israel" they recognized his spiritual leadership of the nation. Although none of Israel's enemies could have kept David out of combat, his own men could.

Like so many leaders, David's active role diminished as he grew older. So, David's success continued by relying more fully on his officers. Delegation of authority was the key to successful management.

DAVID CREDITED OBEDIENCE TO GOD FOR HIS SUCCESS

The scripture records a wonderful song, in which David points to **obedience** as the reason for God's blessings upon his life. "I knew his laws, and I obeyed them. I was perfect in obedience and kept myself from sin. That is why the Lord has done so much for me, for he sees that I am clean."
(2 Samuel 22: 23-25 TLB)

DAVID's LAST WORDS (2 Samuel 1-7, TLB)

These are the last words of David:

David, the son of Jesse, speaks,
David, the man to whom God gave such wonderful success;
David, the anointed of the God of Jacob;

David, sweet psalmist of Israel:
The Spirit of the Lord spoke by me,
And his word was on my tongue.
The Rock of Israel said to me:
One shall come who rules righteously, who rules in the fear of God.
He shall be as the light of the morning; a cloudless sunrise when the tender grass
springs forth upon the earth; As sunshine after rain.'
And it is my family He has chosen! Yes, God has made an everlasting covenant with me;
His agreement is eternal, final, sealed. He will constantly look after my safety and success.
But the godless are as thorns to be thrown away, for they tear the hand that touches them. One must be armed to chop them down; they shall be burned."

Yes, David had the high honor of prophesying the coming of the Messiah. He was also a member of the royal blood line of the Savior. Without question, God created David to serve his purposes on earth.

MIGHTY MEN UNDER DAVID's COMMAND. (From 2 Samuel 23: 8-21)

There were many brave warriors in David's army. The Bible contains an honor role of these mighty men of valor who distinguished themselves in combat with the enemy.

- Adino, the Eznite, who killed 800 men in one battle.

- Eleazar, "one of the three mighty men with David, when they defied the Philistines that were gathered together to battle, and the men of Israel were gone away: He arose, and smote the Philistines until his hand was weary, and his hand clave unto the sword: and the Lord wrought a great victory that day."
- Shammah, despite all others deserting, "stood in the midst of the ground, and defended it, and slew the Philistines: and the Lord wrought a great victory."
- Three of David's top thirty officers broke through the garrison of the Philistines in Bethlehem merely to fetch David a drink of water. This valiant and daring deed caused David to pour the water out as an offering unto the Lord: "Is not this the blood of the men that went in jeopardy of their lives?"
- Abishai, one of the three who had broken through the Philistine lines for David, single-handedly killed 300 enemy soldiers in one encounter.
- Benaiah, who had killed two giants and two lion-like Moabites, also slew a lion in a snowy pit. Additionally, Benaiah, armed only with a staff, wrenched the spear out of the hands of an Egyptian and killed him. Benaiah was the commander of David's bodyguards.

What motivated Benaiah to climb down into a snowy pit to fight a lion? *Because he liked a good fight!* He enjoyed the challenge. Comparing their attitude at this point with when the army had first formed, it is clear that a complete transformation had taken place. Soldiers who had been fearful to leave home had become willing to fight lions just for the sport of it!

DAVID COMMITTED A GRAVE ERROR

Having obtained extraordinary success, David briefly took his eyes off God and focused on himself. He ordered that Joab count the population.

Joab tried to talk him out of it: "God grant that you will live to see the day when there will be a hundred times as many people in your kingdom as there are now! *But you have no right to rejoice in their strength*" (2 Samuel 24:3 TLB). Through many treacherous encounters, Joab had come to know that their successes had never been due to their own strength, size, or intelligence. It was God who had carried them through so many campaigns and dangers. David had nothing to gloat about. But David insisted on taking the census and God sent a plague upon Israel. Because David placed more emphasis on having a large army than on trusting God, God reduced the size of his forces by 70,000 men. God removed the source of pride. Whenever someone or something gets between a believer and God, God will remove it.

However, conducting a national census was an exception in David's life. Normally, David expressed faith in God, trusted in his providence, and recognized the Lord for every victory.

CHARACTERISTICS OF DAVID's LEADERSHIP

We know that David's leadership transformed his men into a great army, but who transformed David into a great leader and what were the ingredients of his leadership?

1. GROOMING

God began to groom David for leadership when he was a youth. Jesse, David's father, had given him responsibility for watching the sheep, and as a shepherd, he learned diligence, oversight, and fighting predators.

When an opportunity arose for David to prove himself publicly, he was confident. Despite the fact that his first enemy encounter was with Goliath, he was well prepared, having already slain a lion and a bear with his own hands. David knew from experience that God would protect him. "The Lord that delivered me out of the paw of the lion, and out of the paw of the bear, he will deliver me out of the hand of this Philistine" (1 Samuel 17:37, KJV).

Following the victory over the giant, David worked directly for Saul and impressed the king so much that he appointed him to be commander of the army. In this capacity, David practiced leadership at the highest level. "And David went out whithersoever Saul sent him, and behaved himself wisely: and Saul set him over the men of war, and he was accepted in the sight of all the people, and also in the sight of Saul's servants" (1 Samuel 18:5).

So, David's entire life prepared him for leadership of Israel. No doubt, God had this in mind all along and David could truly say: "He teaches my hands to war; so that a bow of steel is broken by my arms" (2 Samuel 22:35, KJV). "I follow close behind you, protected by your strong right arm." (Psalms 63:8, TLB)

2. OBEDIENCE and FOLLOWERSHIP

As a youth, David was overlooked for service in the army and was only allowed to fight Goliath because Israel had no other volunteers. In this respect, David knew what it was like to be scorned.

Later, when Saul tried to kill him, David's original 400 recruits could relate to their leader's predicament. They regarded David as "one of us." And he could relate to them, because he also was a follower – of God. Just as God had lifted David from the sheep fields to a position of leadership, David transformed a band of men from the fringes of society into a feared fighting force.

3. EXTRAORDINARY SUBORDINATE LEADERS

David's commanders were cunning men. Joab, his brother Abishai, and Ittaithe the Gittite were all experts in war and brave in the face of danger. They were also able to independently formulate and execute military strategy.

These three commanders spoke to David frankly. On more than one occasion, Joab disagreed with David about leadership and theology. Abishai was quick to express his opinion about killing Saul, and Ittaithe declined David's invitation to return home. He respected their opinions.

In selecting these men, David placed great weight on intellectual attributes. Even though the heroic deeds of "the three" (Adino, Eleazar, and Shammah) exceeded those of their commanders, they were still under the authority of their leaders. Having the greatest fighting skill did not always equate to having the highest rank.

4. DIVERSITY

Some of David's best men were not Israelites. David's army consisted of recruits from many ethnic backgrounds. "And all his servants passed on beside him; and all the Cherethites, and all the Pelethites, and all the Gittites, six hundred men which came after him from Gath, passed on before the king" (2 Samuel 15:18, KJV).

David had learned to examine the inner man of the soldier, not simply how he looked or where he was born. "Man looks on the outward appearance, but the Lord looks on the heart" (2 Samuel 16:7, KJV).

5. LOFTY GOALS

David did not focus on the mundane: he set his sights on great victories. The Bible does not record minor skirmishes involving David. The scriptures recount his great exploits and heroism. David's goals required God's involvement and God responded by doing *great* things in David's life. God working **through** David was far better than David working in his own strength.

Like their leader, David's men also became giant killers. In one of the wars with the Philistines, David's men killed four giants, including Goliath's brother. The army performed exploit after exploit.

- So David and his men went to Keilah, and fought with the Philistines, and brought away their cattle, and smote them with **a great slaughter.** (1 Samuel 23:5)
- And David smote the land, and left neither man nor woman alive, and took away the sheep, and the oxen, and the asses, and the camels, and the apparel, and returned, and came to Achish. (1 Samuel 27:9, KJV)
- Next in rank was Eleazar, the son of Dodo and grandson of Ahohi. He was one of the three men who, with David, held back the Philistines that time when the rest of the Israeli army fled. He killed the Philistines until his hand was too tired to hold his sword; and the Lord gave him **a great victory.** (The rest of the army did not return until it was time to collect the loot!) (2 Samuel 23:9-10, TLB)
- But he stood in the midst of the ground, and defended it, and slew the Philistines: and the Lord wrought **a great victory.**
- And David smote them from the twilight even unto the evening of the next day: and there escaped not a man of them, save four hundred

young men, which rode upon camels, and fled. (1 Samuel 30:17, KJV)

- But again the Syrians fled from the Israelis, this time leaving seven hundred charioteers dead on the field, also forty thousand cavalrymen, including General Shobach (2 Samuel 10:18, TLB).

David did not make small plans. He served the God of the Universe and counted on his supernatural power to perform great exploits. "For by you I have run through a troop: by my God have I leaped over a wall" (2 Samuel 22: 29-30, KJV).

6. PRAYER FIRST

David faced the crazed and demented Saul as well as many other enemies. How did he approach each and every problem? By turning to God before taking action.

David received guidance from the prophet Gad about how to avoid Saul. (1 Samuel 22:5)

- When David got word that the Philistines were attacking Keilah, "*David inquired of the Lord.*" (1 Samuel 23:4, KJV)
- When David learned that Saul was planning to harm him, David asked, "*Bring me the ephod*" (1 Samuel 23:9, KJV). He wanted to adorn himself in priestly attire to ask God for guidance.
- When the Amalekites carried away the families of David's army, "*David inquired of the Lord.*"

God told David to "Pursue: for you shall surely overtake them, and without fail recover all." (1 Samuel 30:8, KJV)

- When Saul and Jonathan died and David wanted to know if he should go to Judah, *"David inquired of the Lord."* And God said, "Unto Hebron." (2 Samuel 2:1, KJV)
- When the Philistines prepared themselves for battle in the valley of Rephaim, *"David inquired of the Lord."* "And the Lord said unto David, 'Go up: for I will doubtless deliver the Philistines into your hand.'" (2 Samuel 5:19, KJV)
- When they attacked a second time, *"David inquired of the Lord"* and received guidance again. (2 Samuel 5:23, KJV)

"Ask of me, and I shall give you the heathen for your inheritance, and the uttermost parts of the earth for your possession" (Psalm 2: 8, KJV).

7. KNOWLEDGE OF ENEMY PLANS AND MOVEMENTS

Any enterprise is built by wise planning, becomes strong through common sense, and profits wonderfully by keeping abreast of the facts. (Proverbs 24: 3-4 TLB)

- When Saul planned to attack David at Keilah, 1 Samuel 23:9 says: "And David knew that Saul secretly practiced mischief against him."

- When Saul pursued David in the wilderness of Maon, 1 Samuel 23:25 records: "And they told David"
- But Jonathan Saul's son delighted much in David: and Jonathan told David, saying, Saul my father seeks to kill you … (1 Samuel 19:2, KJV)
- And there came a messenger to David, saying, 'The hearts of the men of Israel are after Absalom.' (2 Samuel 15:13, KJV)
- And one told David, saying, Ahithophel is among the conspirators with Absalom. (2 Samuel 15:31, KJV)

8. CREDIT TO GOD

David always gave credit to God for each victory. "And Joram brought with him vessels of silver, and vessels of gold, and vessels of brass: Which also King David dedicated unto the Lord, with the silver and gold that he had dedicated of all nations which he subdued …" (2 Samuel 8: 10-11, KJV).

9. THANKGIVING AND HONOR TO GOD

David, skilled musician and composer of Psalms, was a very thankful person. When David's men risked their lives to provide him with a drink from the well in Bethlehem, "he would not drink thereof, but poured it out unto the Lord" (2 Samuel 23:14-16, KJV)

David praised and thanked God for delivering him and blessing him:

"But you are holy, O you that inhabits the praises of Israel. Our fathers trusted in you: they trusted, and you did deliver them" (Psalms 22: 3-4, KJV).

"The Lord lives; and blessed be my rock; and exalted is the God of the rock of my salvation. It is God that avenges me, and that brings down the people under me.

And that brings me forth from my enemies: you also have lifted me up on high above them that rose up against me: you have delivered me from the violent man.

Therefore I will give thanks unto you, O Lord, among the heathen, and I will sing praises unto your name. " (2 Samuel 22: 48-51, KJV).

10. ANNOINTING

Then Samuel took the horn of oil, and anointed him in the midst of his brethren:

"and the Spirit of the Lord came upon David from that day forward." (1 Samuel 16:13)

There is no substitute for the anointing of God. The power, fervor, and help of God is upon the anointed leader.

11. TRUST IN GOD'S CONTROL

Whether at the height of his glory or fleeing for his life, David always knew that God was in control in all situations. "He watches everyone closely" (Psalm 11:4, NLT)

When he was forced to leave Jerusalem, David commented, "If the Lord sees fit … he will bring me back to see the Ark and the Tabernacle again. But if he is through with me, well, let him do what seems best to him" (2 Samuel 15:26 TLB).

As ruler, he understood why God had placed him on the throne. "And David perceived that the Lord had established him king over Israel, and that he had exalted his kingdom *for his people Israel's sake*" (2 Samuel 5:12, KJV).

Ready

To defend God's honor, I accepted readily
My faith is certain and growing steadily.

He is full of insults and reproaches
I see anger and disdain as he approaches.

I am young, slender and ruddy
And mortal combat has been his life's study

I have not reached full frame nor height
And he has known victory in every fight

Yet his armor, sword and shield are misplaced
I am not like the others he has faced

No, this is not a battle between men
He is dueling with God because of his sin.

The outcome is certain despite his array
I will behead him this very day

They questioned my ability to handle this chore
But I have killed a lion and bear before.

God protected me from their paws
So with this one who has defied his laws.

My leather pouch holds stones that kill.
A shepherd has time to hone his skill.

His heavy armor is thick and covers so well,
But there's a way this giant to fell.

Running toward him, I take the offensive.
His unprotected head will prove expensive.

Out of my sling the weapon flies to its mark.
Immediately finding his forehead so stark.

A crash to the earth announces his fate.
Judgment for looking upon us with hate.

An heroic deed was done this day.
God saved Israel in his unusual way.

The hour required one who would not fear it.
Calling for faith and things of the spirit.

Just a shepherd, yes, only a youth
But savvy enough to know God's truth.

David and the Armies of the Living God

A Study in Transformational Leadership

QUESTIONS TO CONSIDER

---

1) **The Bible tells us that God had departed from King Saul and was with David.**

   a) Is God's favor the determining factor in success or failure?
   b) How would you obtain God's favor?
   c) What were David's motives in leading Israel?

2) **What does popularity have to do with leadership?**

   a) Have you ever seen a team go "from worst to first" when a new coach came in?
   b) Was the leader popular when he or she first arrived?
   c) What does leadership have to do with the success of a team?
   d) How much responsibility for success do leaders have? (Express in %).
   e) How much responsibility for success do team members have? (Express in %).

3) **When you commit yourself to a team or project, do you also pledge your loyalty?**

a) What is loyalty?
b) Should loyalty go both ways?

4) As David grew old, he relied more on his subordinate leaders?

a) To protect David from being captured or killed, his soldiers advised him to use his subordinates more. What does this tell you about their esteem for David?
b) This practice proved to be successful on the battlefield. In what other ways did this help Israel as a nation?

5) David committed a great blunder when he counted all the citizens under his command. Why did God become angry about this? What did God do about David's pride? 2 Samuel 24:15

"So the LORD sent a pestilence upon Israel from the morning even to the time appointed: and there died of the people from Dan even to Beer-sheba seventy thousand men."

6) Why does the Bible focus on David's great exploits?

a) Wasn't his routine leadership noteworthy?
b) In athletics, there is a saying, "It's not what you do, it's when you do it." Is timing everything?
c) A great coach said, "Practice does not make perfect. perfect practice makes perfect." The nerves in throughout your body have a lining,

or sheath, around them. When you perform a task the same way over and over, this lining thickens to reinforce the repeated behavioral pattern. This creates a "habit" of repeating the behavior, whether good or bad. Is the phrase, "Do your best" more than just routine encouragement?

7) **David kept an eye on his enemies through informants (1 Samuel 19:2, 1 Samuel 23:9, 1 Samuel 23:25, 2 Samuel 15:13, and 2 Samuel 15:31). Today, corporations spend vast sums of money to learn what competitors are doing.**

   a) Is this ethical?
   b) Is this necessary to survive?
   c) How do organizations prosper? "Any enterprise is built by wise planning, becomes strong through common sense, and profits wonderfully by keeping abreast of the facts. (Proverbs 24:3-4)
   d) What are the dangers of not knowing what your competitors are planning?

8) **David's battles were sandwiched in between prayer and praise: prayer for victory in the beginning and praise for victory afterwards.**

   a) Is prayer more important than praise? Why or why not?
   May the nations praise you, O God. Yes, may all the nations praise you.

<u>Then the earth will yield its harvests, and God, our God, will richly bless us.</u> (Psalm 67:5-6, TLB)

b) Does praise bring God's presence? "But you are holy, O you that inhabits the praises of Israel." (Psalm 22:3)

c) If you ask the LORD to lead your team, will He accept?

David and the Armies of the Living God

A Study in Transformational Leadership

DISCUSSION QUESTIONS AND ACTIVITIES

Top Gun

Each attendee is invited to identify the most important attribute of a leader.

Record these on the board. Discuss.

Objective: To identify the leadership traits that inspire.

Mixed Emotions

In small groups, discuss the following questions:

Have you been in a situation in which you were expected to show loyalty to an overbearing supervisor?

- How did you respond?
- What was the ultimate outcome?

Objective: To consider ethical issues of leadership and loyalty and to promote moral behavior in trying circumstances.

A Man for All Seasons

David was a king, shepherd, singer, writer, warrior, family man, teacher, judge and statesman. What are the advantages of having a blend of gifts and talents in a leader?

Is leadership an art, a science, or both?

In what situations are "soft skills" important?

How important are technical skills for a leader?

Objective: To recognize talents in leaders and how they contribute to success.

What talents do you have that help you in leadership positions?

Which do you rely on most often?

Class Discussion: Make hay while the sun is shining.

- What does a sense of timing have to do with success?
- What does timing have to do with communications?
- Is it better to be too early or too late?

Objective: To consider the quality and the **timing** of their actions.

Small Group Discussion: Plenty of Experience in the Field

David was a shepherd in his early life.

- How did being a shepherd groom David for leadership?
- What kinds of predators are in your work area?
- Are there any threats to your work?
- Can you categorize these into emotional, financial, spiritual, physical?
- Can success be dangerous?
- Is it harder to handle success than adversity? Why?
- What is the main duty of a shepherd?
- Does this take the most time?
- Does shepherding require a certain amount of ease with yourself?

- How are people like sheep?

Objective: To think about subtle threats to your success, such as wasting time.

From your study of David, what is your most important "take away?"

Each attendee is invited to answer the following question:

Which of David's leadership practices is the most applicable and important in your life?

Record the answers on the board and then rank them by popular vote.

Objective:

To share and reinforce the most important lesson learned from David's life.

CHAPTER 4

SOLOMON AND HIS BRIDE

A Study in Love

**I would still be worth nothing at all without love.
(1 Corinthians 13:2, TLB)**

There once was a king who wore a crown that his mother had given him on his wedding day, "*the day of his gladness*" (Song 3:11, KJV). The king was handsome, popular, and world famous for his wisdom. His wife was also stunning, but she had spent a great deal of time working in the vineyards and felt that her beauty had faded. The king, however, saw nothing except perfect loveliness and he was completely smitten by this young lady.

Their love ballad, "The Song of Solomon," expressed their most cherished feelings, chambered deeply within their hearts. Their reflections upon the memories they shared reveal the devotion and passion they had for each other.

The queen was completely enamored with the king. To enhance her beauty, she adorned herself artfully with the sparkling, polished jewels and smooth, silk apparel. She fit right into his plans, all the while longing for quiet moments alone with him. And the queen perfumed herself with aromas so intoxicating that the king rested in the serenity of her arms, enthralled by her charms and delighted by her every word.

King Solomon expressed his love for her in intimate ways. He praised her beauty, describing her cheeks "with rows of jewels" and her neck "with chains of gold" (Song of Solomon 1:10, KJV). Her stunning glory only made him want to shower her with more adornment, and he added "golden earrings and silver beads" (Song 1:11, TLB). He continued to lavish compliments on her, comparing her to a fragrant bouquet of flowers, delightful to his eyes and sweet to his senses.

When he garnished such praise upon his bride, it felt like fresh soft rain to her, gently soaking her from her crowned hair to the soles of her adorned feet. Oh, how her heart soared! She was so honored to be King Solomon's queen that she sang joyfully, "He brought me to the banqueting house, and his banner over me was love" (Song 2: 4, KJV).

She became faint from the great attention the king devoted to her. He focused on her and her alone. "His left hand is under my head, and his right hand embraces me" (Song 2:6).

Although she cherished his passion desperately, she never demanded his attention or hurried him. "I charge you, Oh, daughters of Jerusalem, by the roes, and by the hinds of the field, that you stir not up, nor awake my love, <u>till he please</u>" (Song 2:7, KJV). She never pressured him because love does not demand its own way. (1 Corinthians 13). She was content to wait patiently for the king. And he never disappointed her. Soon she heard an unmistakable, familiar voice, and her heart leapt. She saw his striking silhouette, drawing nearer and nearer, and she could only cheer his prowess as he raced to her. "Ah, I hear him-my beloved! Here he comes, leaping upon the mountains and bounding over the hills. My beloved is like a gazelle or young deer" (Song 2:9, TLB). With utmost delight, she heard the unforgettable invitation that thrilled every fiber in her body and sent every recess of her soul into ecstasy: "Arise, my love, my fair one, and come away" (Song 2:13, KJV). Her fondest hope was now certain, her most fantastic dream had become reality.

The only thing that mattered to her was him. "My beloved is mine, and I am his" (Song 2:16, KJV).

Her astonishing loveliness mesmerized the king. He took time to point out the perfection of each part of her body: her glistening eyes, shimmery hair, sparkling teeth, enchanting lips, sculptured head and neck, and her enticing bosom. He also commented on a special treasure of her personality and intellect, her beautiful speech.

She exceeded his highest physical and emotional desires. "I am overcome by one glance of your eyes, by a single bead of your necklace" (Song 4:9, TLB). The king told her that he was held "captive in your queenly tresses" (Song 7:5, TLB).

He also delighted in her faithfulness to him. "My darling bride is like a private garden, a spring that no one else can have, a fountain of my own." (Song 4:12, KJV).

The king was not the only one who was mesmerized by the aura of his beloved. The queen was thoroughly swept away by her husband's glorious looks as well. She extolled the handsome features of the king: "My beloved one is tanned and handsome, better than ten thousand others! His head is purest gold, and he has wavy, raven hair. His eyes are like doves beside the water brooks, deep and quiet. His cheeks are like sweetly scented beds of spices. His lips are perfumed lilies, his breath like myrrh. His arms are round bars of gold set with topaz; his body is bright ivory encrusted with jewels. His legs are as pillars of marble set in sockets of finest gold, like cedars of Lebanon; none can rival him. His mouth is altogether sweet, lovable in every way. Such, O women of Jerusalem, is my beloved, my friend." (Song of Solomon 5:10-16, TLB).

Her last comment is so revealing. She called the king "*my friend.*" She trusted him with her confidences and shared casual, light-hearted moments of fun. Their relationship included the ordinary things of life; walking through flowery fields, a refreshing drink from a chilly spring, and resting quietly under a shade tree.

They never took one another for granted and cherished their intimacy. She carefully selected a quiet hour and place to be alone together, "Let us get up early to the vineyards; let us see if the vine flourish, whether the tender grape appear, and the pomegranates bud forth: there will I give you my loves" (Song 7:12). And she prepared delightful gifts for him. "The mandrakes give a smell, and at our gates are all manner of pleasant fruits, new and old, which I have laid up for you, O my beloved" (Song 7:13, KJV).

The lovely lady had resolved to be loyal to her king for the rest of her life. Only strong love could account for such devotion. She gave him something that no amount of gold could buy: her heart. "Set me in your heart with permanent betrothal, for *love is strong as death* … If a man tried to buy it with everything he owned, he couldn't do it" (Song of Solomon 8: 6-7, TLB).

These two were in love, love that was as strong as death. They treasured one another. They fit together in all situations and at all times, knowing life as only two united souls can. They were vibrant, happy, and generous.

Without love, there would have been a story, but not a song; a couple, but not an item. Without love, their relationship would have been a journey, but not a celebration.

Theirs is not a tale, but a romantic dream come true.

Solomon and His Bride: A Study of Love

QUESTIONS TO CONSIDER

---

1) How important are good relationships to happiness in life?

2) Is it possible to love a cause or an ideal? If so, why?

3) If you fell in love with an ideal or mission,

   a) How would you talk about it?
   b) How would you treat others with the same beliefs?
   c) What do you express commitment?
   d) How do you maintain long term relationships?
   e) Is it possible to offend family members?

4) Can you name three different types of love?

5) Can love ever end?

6) Have you ever known two people who loved one another?

   a) How did it affect their lives?
   b) What quality did the relationship add to their lives?

7) Is there such a thing as love at first sight?

8) Can two people who are totally different love one another?

9) Is self-love healthy or unhealthy?

10) What is the difference between esteem and love?

11) Is love or selfless?

12) How can you tell that a person loves someone or something?

13) Does love foster concern for the well-being of others?

14) Is love a decision or a feeling?

15) What is the opposite of love? Hate? Apathy?

Solomon and His Bride: A Study of Love
DISCUSSION QUESTIONS AND ACTIVITIES

Open Class Discussion: "Favorite Subjects."

What courses did you love in school? Why?

What type of work do you love? Why?

Objective:
To introduce the topic of love.

Open Class Discussion: Is love earned?

Objective:
To examine emotions in relationships.

Open Class Discussion: Does love motivate?

For example, would love for family fuel performance?

Objective:
To consider how relationships affects actions.

Open Class Discussion: How can you tell when someone is in love?

What behavior reveals that someone is in love?

How do people express love?

List them on the board.

For example, giving, helping, communicating, touching.

If you love your job, how do you feel about expending maximum energy in it?

Objectives:

- To understand that love affects **what we do**.
- To identify selfish and selfless conduct and attitudes.

CHAPTER 5

Elijah and Elisha

A Study in Apprenticeship

I will not leave you. (2 Kings 2:2, KJV)

Elijah and his apprentice Elisha both knew that Almighty God was about to sweep Elijah into eternity. Though a master among prophets, Elijah himself had always been astonished by his student Elisha's steadfast devotion. Elisha treasured every word spoken by Elijah and followed him wherever he went.

Now, once again, they found themselves in their usual circumstance: close together and apart from the others. God's next appointed destination for Elijah was heaven. But God's next assignment for Elisha was a world without Elijah.

Although Elijah stood at the door of heaven, his mind was on his son in the ministry. How can the inseparable part? What farewell fits the loss of mentor, friend, and inspiration? Elijah was the one person on earth who had been there from the first call of Elisha to this very day: through miraculous displays of power and in the mundane tasks of daily life; through prophecy and small talk; fire from heaven and campfires in the desert. There was only one soul on earth that close to Elisha, and he was leaving, for the rest of his earthly life.

Moses could have passed on a staff and David could have bequeathed a harp. But what do you offer someone whose most prized treasure is yourself? Elijah wanted to give Elisha the desire of his heart, but what could that be? "Ask what I shall do for you, before I am taken away from you." There was no need for Elisha to ponder the question because he had known all along what he wanted: "I pray you, let a double portion of your spirit be upon me" (2 Kings 2:9, KJV). The request teetered on the brink of recreation, and took the great Elijah back for a moment. Nonetheless, this supernatural petition fit his favorite pupil perfectly and was the natural next step.

Of course, that was it! Elisha wanted to be twice as much like Elijah as Elijah himself!

The request honored and thrilled Elijah. Throughout his career as God's spokesman, Elijah had foretold many events, but he could not guarantee God's answer, or the farewell that was about to unfold. So Elijah told Elisha that his request would be granted if he saw "the chariot of Israel, and the horsemen thereof" (2 Kings 2:12, KJV). Lo and behold, Elisha saw God's heavenly escort appear in the sky carrying Elijah to his heavenly home. Elisha tore his robe in grief and then "picked up Elijah's cloak and returned to the bank of the Jordan River, and struck the water with it. 'Where is the Lord God of Elijah?' he cried out. And the water parted and Elisha went across!" (2 Kings 2:14, TLB). The double anointing was upon him and a ministry of power before him.

Elisha had pursued Elijah to his last earthly breath and received an awesome blessing. God saves the best for last. Elisha was now doubly equipped to carry on in Elijah's place. What a disciple! What a follower! Now, what a mighty man of God!

What about students and teachers today? Students pick which teachers they want based on how much homework is required, how funny they are, and when the class is offered. They evaluate and grade teachers. If the student makes a bad grade, then it's the teacher's fault.

But how much responsibility for learning do students have? Are students in class to learn or simply to complete a required course? They watch for the slightest misstep by the teacher, yet overlook their own lack of initiative. They focus on getting an A more than getting an education. Do any realize that the teacher's job is not to spoon feed them? Has the drive to complete a degree surpassed the desire to learn?

Likewise, do workers train under a master craftsman to learn how to do quality work? Or, are they trying to obtain a certification that they can put on their resumes?

Elisha attained through followership. He started by "carrying the bags," but finished as chief of the prophets. Elisha made it his business to be where

Elijah was. He learned by hanging around. He learned by participating. He learned by doing. He learned by paying attention. He learned by observation and revelation. He learned by others' mistakes and his own mistakes. He learned by asking questions and making comments. He learned by reading and by listening. He learned by imitating the teacher. He learned by passing up opportunities elsewhere in order to spend time with his teacher. He learned any way he could at any time he could. He learned by doing.

Elisha was the super glue of ancient times. He had much in common with Elijah's shadow. In fact, he was Elijah's shadow. The other prophets never had to ask where Elisha was because he was always in the same place: **near to the source of wisdom**.

Do Christians have such a desire today? Are we willing to abandon the entertainment and activities of the world in order to be with Jesus? Nobody can be in two places at the same time.

Likewise, in the New Testament, Mary, chose to sit at Jesus' feet rather than help her sister Martha. When Martha complained, the Lord said "Only one thing is important. Mary has made the right choice, and it will never be taken away from her." (Luke 10:42, NKJV). Mary turned from the hustle and bustle of mundane chores to hear the words of Jesus. A wise decision!

When the opportunity to learn presents itself, take it.

Elisha and Elijah: A Study in Apprenticeship
QUESTIONS TO CONSIDER

1) **Elijah probably recognized that Elisha was an exceptional student. Did this make the other students feel less important?**

2) **Why was Elisha so desperate to learn everything he could from Elijah?**

   a) How much time do you have to devote acquire skills to succeed?
   b) Does your mentor have experience that could change your career for the better?

3) **Did Elijah test Elisha?**

   a) How so?
   b) How often should people be tested?
   c) What type of tests do you like? Why?
   d) Do you do better when you work alone or with others?

4) **Which of the following describes being a teacher?**

   a) Fun
   b) Demanding.
   c) Something you might like to do.

d) Draining.
e) Rewarding.
f) Satisfying
g) Invigorating

5) How do you feel about the following learning formats?

a) On-the-job training
b) On-line classes.
c) Professional reading.
d) Seminars
e) Apprenticeships
f) Internships
g) Mentorships
h) In person brick-and-mortar classroom instruction.

Elijah and Elisha: A Study in Apprenticeship

DISCUSSION QUESTIONS AND ACTIVITIES

Small Group Interaction: The More You Know, the More You Grow

Your learning and improvement can come from a number of sources.

What per cent of the responsibility for your learning falls on the following?

- Your peers, mentor, supervisor, or teacher.
- Technology.
- Text books.
- Yourself. Is self-discovery the highest form of learning?
- Divine revelation.

Group may draw a pie on the board with a "slice" for each percentage.

Reconvene and discuss.

Objective: To recognized the many opportunities to grow and learn.

Discussion: Priorities

Elijah had a very limited list of priorities.

What does this mean to you?

Objective: To consider how focus applies to learning.

Class Discussion: Success as a function of drive.

Was Elisha's success a function of his astounding intellect or his drive to learn?

Did you know that the brain has tremendous "elasticity" throughout your life?

This elasticity allows you to adapt and learn different things at any point in life.

Objective: To consider drive, desire, and "the human factor" in learning.

Group Interaction: The Proof is in the Pudding.

Discuss how Elijah knew that he had taught Elisha well.

Objective: Clarify the definition of success in teaching and learning.

CHAPTER 6

DANIEL AND HIS FRIENDS

A Study in Deliverance

**For the eyes of the Lord run to and fro
throughout the whole earth,
to show himself *strong* in the behalf of them
whose heart is perfect toward him.
2 Chronicles 16:9**

During the reign of King Nebuchadnezzar, Iraq defeated Israel and took captive a number of Israelite children from the tribe of Judah, sons of Israel's royal family. He intended to develop them into as advisors. The king directed a superintendent to select youth who were well educated, impressive, and poised.

Iraqi Indoctrination

The superintendent chose a number of these young men including Daniel and his three companions called Shadrach, Meshach, and Abednego. One of the first things prescribed for them was a rich diet of the very best Iraqi food. This presented a problem, however, because the young Jewish captives only ate food approved by their Jewish laws.

Daniel approached the superintendent, who had a fondness for Daniel, about not eating from the Iraqi menu them. The superintendent was apprehensive about allowing Daniel to eat only vegetables and water as he requested. But Daniel negotiated wisely and won approval for a ten-day trial period without the rich palace foods.

After ten days, Daniel and his three friends were stronger and much healthier than any of those who had accepted the king's food. Thus, Daniel and his companions separated themselves unto God from the beginning.

God Gave Special Ability to Learn

God blessed these four young Jews intellectually and they quickly learned everything they were taught. Not only that, God gave Daniel a special gift of understanding the meaning of dreams and visions. This gift would later bring Daniel great honor and prove that Daniel's God knew all things.

After interviewing them extensively, King Nebuchadnezzar appointed them as advisors. And their counsel to the king was much more helpful than any other.

The King's Dream

One night the king had a dream which troubled him greatly. However, he could not remember the dream, let alone the meaning of the dream. When he inquired of the usual group of magicians and fortune tellers, none of them could reveal anything about the dream. So Nebuchadnezzar commanded that all of his wise men be executed.

When the officer in charge of the executions came to Daniel, Daniel asked why there was such a great uproar. When he heard about the dream, Daniel again bargained for a little time to provide an answer to the king.

Daniel immediately met with his three friends, those who had also refused the Iraqi food in order to remain true to their faith. They all earnestly prayed to God to reveal both the king's dream and its meaning. While Daniel was sleeping soundly that night, God gave him a vision that explained the mysterious dream. When Daniel understood the vision, he praised God with this beautiful oration:

> "Blessed be the name of God forever and ever, for he alone has all wisdom and all power. World events are under his control. He removes kings and sets others on their thrones. He gives wise men their wisdom, and scholars their intelligence. He reveals profound mysteries beyond man's understanding. He knows all hidden things, for he is

light, and darkness is no obstacle to him. I thank and praise you, O God of my fathers, for you have given me wisdom and glowing health, and now, even this vision of the king's dream, and the understanding of what it means" (Daniel 2: 20-23, TLB).

After thanking and praising God, Daniel went to see the king and told him that he was ready to reveal the dream and its interpretation. But Daniel refused to take any credit for his understanding and made it clear that God had revealed the meaning of the dream. Then Daniel explained that the king had dreamed about a tall statue of a man, made from various metals and clay. Furthermore, that the head of the statue represented his own kingdom, while the other parts represented future kingdoms. Finally, the feet represented the last worldly government, which would be destroyed by God's kingdom which would never end.

King Nebuchadnezzar was overwhelmed by Daniel's explanation and fell to the ground. He also stated that Daniel's God was "the God of gods, Ruler of kings, the Revealer of mysteries" (Daniel 2:47, KJV). He put Daniel in charge of the Kingdom and all his counselors, and bestowed many gifts upon him.

Daniel showed loyalty by promoting his three friends, Shadrach, Meshach, and Abednego. They served faithfully as his closest confidants and advisors.

Nebuchadnezzar Builds an Idol to Worship (Daniel, Chapter 3)

King Nebuchadnezzar constructed a huge idol and commanded everyone in Iraq to bow before it. The governors, judges, and other officials of the empire followed the king's command. But Daniel and his three friends did not. Seeing this, some of the other officials brought an accusation against Shadrach, Meshach, and Abednego.

The angry king confronted them.

> "'Is it true, O Shadrach, Meshach, and Abednego' he asked, 'that you are refusing to serve my gods or to worship the golden statue I set up? I'll give you one more chance. When the music plays, if you fall down and worship the statue, all will be well. But if you refuse, you will be thrown into a flaming furnace within the hour. And what god can deliver you out of my hands then?'" (Daniel 3: 14-15, TLB).

Notice Nebuchadnezzar's last statement, *"And what god can deliver you out of my hands then?"* This arrogant king unwittingly challenged Almighty God. Shadrach, Meshach, and Abednego were unbending before the king and expressed no concern about being burned alive. They replied, *"O Nebuchadnezzar, we are not worried about what will happen to us"* (Daniel 3:16, TLB).

Their statement reveals absolute confidence in God. They had walked with God their entire lives and they knew that God would never abandon them. They were bold because they understood that God controls everything – even the fiery flames of a furnace!

They continued: "If we are thrown into the flaming furnace, our God is able to deliver us; and he will deliver us out of your hand, Your Majesty. But if he doesn't, please understand, sir, that even then we will never under any circumstance serve your gods or worship the golden statue you have erected." (Daniel 3: 17-18, TLB)

These young men had determined that they would remain loyal to God. They would not defile themselves by bowing to an idol. Although they lived in Iraq, they were citizens of heaven. They had chosen to be set apart for God. And they were prepared to die if necessary, knowing that death would only bring new life in their eternal home with God. They were much like Job when he said, "Though he slay me, yet will I trust in him." (Job 13:15, KJV).

To destroy the three Jewish princes, he made the fire much hotter than usual. He also selected very able guards to tie Shadrach, Meshach, and Abednego with ropes and toss them into the furnace. When they did, the raging flames leapt out and killed the soldiers! And the three friends fell into the roaring flames, bound hand and foot.

In a moment, King Nebuchadnezzar saw something he would never forget: a fourth figure walked about in the flames with the princes, who were no longer tied. None of them were consumed or disturbed by the fire, content to commune together! And the fourth man looked Divine!

The king shouted to Shadrach, Meshach, and Abednego to come forth from the fire. Although the ropes were completely destroyed, their clothes and hair were not singed, and there was no smell of smoke. All the officials present examined them and were astonished!

A Heathen King Honors God and His Servants

Stunned by this miracle of deliverance, King Nebuchadnezzar praised God:

> "Blessed be the God of Shadrach, Meshach, and Abednego, for he sent his angel to deliver his trusting servants when they defied the king's commandment, and were willing to die rather than serve or worship any god except their own. Therefore, I make this decree, that any person of any nation, language, or religion who speaks a word against the God of Shadrach, Meshach, and Abednego shall be torn limb from limb and his house knocked into a heap of rubble. For no other God can do what this one does." (Daniel 3:28-29, TLB).

What a reversal by the once boastful king! The same Nebuchadnezzar that challenged God now praised him! Then, the king bestowed promotions on Shadrach, Meshach, and Abednego. And prosperity accompanied the three foreigners in Iraq.

King Nebuchadnezzar Has Another Dream (Daniel, Chapter 4)

One night, King Nebuchadnezzar had another dream which he could not interpret. Again, none of his magicians, astrologers, or fortune tellers could explain its meaning. But Daniel was summoned and the king told him the details of his dream. The king related that, in the mysterious dream, a great tree had been cut down but its stump left in place, exposed to the elements. In the dream, an angel announced:

> "For seven years let him have the mind of an animal instead of a man. For this has been decreed by the Watchers, demanded by the Holy Ones. The purpose of this decree is that all the world may understand that the Most High dominates the kingdoms of the world, and gives them to anyone he wants to, even the lowliest of men!" (Daniel 4: 16-17, TLB)

The meaning of the dream was perfectly clear to Daniel and he was startled by it. Daniel could not even speak for an hour. Finally, the king assured Daniel that it was all right to tell him the meaning of the dream. So, Daniel, with deep respect, told King Nebuchadnezzar that the great tree represented the king himself, and its falling meant that he would lose his kingdom. Furthermore, the king would lose his mind for seven years, eating the grass of the fields and living like an animal. But at the end of seven years, he would be restored to his throne. The purpose of this experience was to teach Nebuchadnezzar that God rules the kingdoms of the world and gives them to whomever he wishes.

All of this began a year later, when a voice from heaven spoke to the king as he walked upon the roof of his royal palace:

> "O King Nebuchadnezzar, this message is for you: You are no longer ruler of this kingdom. You will be forced out of the palace to live with the animals in the fields, and to eat grass like the cows for seven years until you finally realize that <u>God parcels out the kingdoms of men</u> and gives them to anyone he chooses." (Daniel 4: 31-32, TLB)

For seven years, Nebuchadnezzar lived in the wild. His hair grew long and coarse and his fingernails became like an eagle's claws. His body was damp with dew and he ate the grass of the field. Seven years later, he looked up to heaven and his sanity was restored. His honor, kingdom, counselors, and subjects returned also. He praised and thanked God, proclaiming God's dominion over all the earth: "All the people of the earth are nothing when compared to him; he does whatever he thinks best among the hosts of heaven, as well as here among the inhabitants of earth." (Daniel 4:35, TLB)

Daniel Reveals Judgment to a New King (Daniel, Chapter 5)

Later, after Nebuchadnezzar's reign ended, a man named Belshazzar became king. One day this new ruler hosted a large feast for 1,000 of his officers. Belshazzar called for the sacred cups, which were taken from the Jewish Temple of Jerusalem long ago, so that he and his associates could drink wine from them. So the attendants brought them to the party and they were used to offer toasts to idols.

But even as they drank, a man's fingers appeared mysteriously and wrote on the wall before the king. He was horrified by this sight and immediately called for his advisors to interpret the writing. The king also offered lavish gifts and a position of great authority to anyone who could explain the writing. However, neither the mystics, nor the astrologers, nor the occultists could read the message. So the king and his officers descended into panic and confusion.

When the queen mother heard about the upheaval, she found the king and consoled him by telling him that there was an old man in the kingdom who could solve the issue: Daniel. So Daniel was rushed in to see the king.

Although the king offered Daniel gifts, he refused to accept them. Yet he agreed to explain the writing on the wall. He gave a lengthy but crushing explanation to the king:

> "Your Majesty, the Most High God gave Nebuchadnezzar, who long ago preceded you, a kingdom and majesty and glory and honor. He gave him such majesty that all the nations of the world trembled before him in fear. He killed any who offended him, and spared any he liked. At his whim they rose or fell. But when his heart and mind were hardened in pride, God removed him from his royal throne and took away his glory, and he was chased out of his palace into the fields, His thoughts and feelings became those of an animal, and he lived among the wild donkeys; he ate grass like the cows and his body was wet with the dew of heaven, until at last he knew that <u>the Most High overrules the kingdoms of men</u>, and that he appoints anyone he desires to reign over them.
>
> And you, his successor, O Belshazzar – you knew all this, yet you have not been humble. For you have defied the Lord of Heaven, and brought here these cups from his Temple; and you and your officers and wives and concubines have been drinking wine from them while praising gods of silver, gold, brass, iron,

wood, and stone-gods that neither see nor hear, nor know anything at all. But you have not praised the God who gives you the breath of life and controls your destiny! And so God sent those fingers to write this message: 'Mene,' 'Mene,' 'Tekel,' 'Parsin.' This is what it means:

"Mene means 'numbered' – God has numbered the days of your reign, and they are ended. "Tekel means 'weighed' – you have been weighed in God's balances and have failed the test. "Parsin means 'divided' – your kingdom will be divided and given to the Medes and Persians." (Daniel 5: 18-30, TLB)

The interpretation devastated the king, but he realized that everything spoken by Daniel was true. So he provided Daniel with a purple robe, a golden chain, and the third highest position in the kingdom.

That night, the king died.

Daniel Serves Another New Ruler (Daniel, Chapter 6)

A Mede by the name of Darius entered Iraq and assumed the throne. When the new king began to exercise his authority, he named Daniel to be one of three rulers immediately under him. Daniel had many governors under him, and in this high position, Daniel excelled, earning the king's highest recognition.

When the king began to consider appointing Daniel over the other rulers, they began to search for some fault in him. However, there was nothing of which to accuse Daniel because he lieved with absolute integrity. His jealous peers then began to focus on his religion.

Knowing that Daniel was utterly loyal to God, the other rulers devised a plan to create a conflict in loyalty between the David's God and the king. So, they obtained the king's signature on a decree that prohibited anyone from asking a favor from God, or any man, except the king. This order was to remain in effect for 30 days and, as a law of the Medes and Persians, could not be rescinded for any reason at all.

Daniel, of course, had no intention of breaking his allegiance to God and continued to pray three times a day in full view of anyone passing by. Seeing this, the officials raced back to the king to report Daniel's activity.

When the king heard this, he was quite upset that he had been manipulated by his officials. He tried desperately failed to find a way to avoid condemning Daniel. He finally agreed to have him arrested and thrown to the lions.

The guards threw Daniel into the lions' den and placed a stone over the entry, sealed with the king's ring. No one in Iraq would dare remove the stone. So the king left Daniel in the lions' den, but he himself stayed awake all night. Very early in the morning, he rushed to the lions' den and called for Daniel. And to the king's great relief, Daniel answered: "Your Majesty, live forever! My God has sent his angel to shut the lions' mouths so that they can't touch me; for I am innocent before God, nor, sir, have I wronged you." (Daniel 6:21, TLB)

And not a scratch was found on him, because he believed in his God. (Daniel (6:23, TLB). How reminiscent of the time his three friends were thrown into the fiery pit! They had come forth without a hair burned and now Daniel emerged without a scratch! What a protective, all-powerful God!

Then the king threw Daniel's accusers, and their families, into the den. The vicious lions ripped them apart in mid-air.

And just as King Nebuchadnezzar had praised the God for protecting Shadrach, Meshach, and Abednego, now King Darius gave God credit for sending an angel to protect Daniel. This is history's only recorded reversal of a law of the Medes and the Persians:

> "Greetings! I decree that everyone shall tremble and fear before the God of Daniel in every part of my kingdom. For his God is the living, unchanging God whose kingdom shall never be destroyed and whose power shall never end. *He delivers his people*, preserving them from harm; he does great miracles in heaven and earth; it *is he who delivered Daniel from the power of the lions*." **(Daniel 6: 26-27, TLB).**

One day, we may all need this kind of faith.

And they overcame him by the blood of the Lamb, and by the word of their testimony; and they loved not their lives unto the death. (Revelation 12:11)

Daniel and His Three Friends

A Study in Deliverance

QUESTIONS TO ASK YOURSELF

---

1) **Daniel, Shadrach, Meshach, and Abednego were Jewish captives in a land with different religious beliefs. Yet, they maintained integrity.**

   a) At times, do you feel pressured to cut corners or overlook wrongdoing?
   b) Is the pressure often related to deadlines?

2) **In the book of Daniel, we learn that King Nebuchadnezzar demanded that Daniel's three friends worship a man-made statue. When they refused, the king threatened to throw them into the fire. Yet, they would not bow to the idol, so, the guards threw them into the fiery furnace.**

   a) Would you be willing to die for your beliefs?
   b) Would you be willing to lose your job for your convictions?

3) **King Nebuchadnezzar became arrogant and God caused him to lose his mind for seven years. During this time, he lived like an animal in the fields. The New Testament, in James 4:6,**

tells us that "God resists the proud, but gives grace unto the humble."

    a) Do you recognize that your intellect, skills, and opportunities all come from God?

    b) Do you feel that you can get along without God?

4) **Is it possible to come into conflict because you are a friend of God?**

5) **Is it possible to come into conflict because you are a friend of some people?**

6) **Later, Darius entered Iraq and assumed the throne. Soon thereafter, some evil men hatched a scheme to trap Daniel for practicing his faith. Daniel continued to pray and observe his faith, so King Darius threw him into the lion's den. However, God preserved Daniel's life, but killed his accusers, who were ripped apart by the lions.**

    a) If Daniel knew that God would <u>not</u> save his life from the lions, would he have maintained his religious beliefs?

    b) Have you ever seen perpetrators set a trap, only to fall into it themselves?

    c) There is an old saying, "What goes around, comes around." Is there divine justice?

        i) Jesus asked, "And shall not God avenge his own elect, which cry day and night unto him, though he bear long with them? I tell

you that he will avenge them **speedily**."
(Luke 18:7-8).

ii) "Seeing *it is* a <u>**righteous**</u> thing with God
to recompense tribulation to them that
trouble you." (2 Thessalonians 1:6).

iii) In life, do you harvest what you plant?

Daniel and His Three Friends

A Study in Deliverance

GROUP DISCUSSION / ACTIVITIES

Values: *Taught or Caught?*

Although Daniel, Shadrach, Meshach, and Abednego may not have preached to the Iraqi people every morning, their actions spoke louder than words.

Does your "walk" speak louder than your "talk"?

Objective: To examine the power of setting a good example.

Discussion: Martyrs

Have the class name as many martyrs, Christian, patriotic, or other, as they can.

List them on the board and invite comments on each.

Objective: To introduce the topic of ethics in our lives and work.

Discussion: Are we consistent?

What would you think of someone who is cordial, fair, and kind to her employees at work, but abusive of her children at home?

What would you think about a man who is in charge of 1,000 people, but who cannot keep a family together?

Invite discussion about being consistently ethical in all circumstances.

Objective: To encourage morality in every area of life.

Discussion: The Enforcer

How much responsibility does the manager or mentor have to enforce integrity?

How much individual responsibility do you have for integrity?

Objective: To cultivate honesty.

CHAPTER 7

MORDECAI AND ESTHER

A Study in Taking Risks

If I perish, I perish. (Esther 4:16, KJV)

In ancient times, the Jews were dispersed throughout the Middle East. One of these kingdoms was Media-Persia, with a vast dominion ranging from Ethiopia to India.

The king of this domain was married to a beautiful queen named Vashti. The king held a great feast, with plenty of fine wine, extravagant entertainment, and many guests. In the presence of all his dignitaries, officials, and military commanders, the king summoned his lovely queen. But, to his surprise, she refused to come.

This embarrassed the king severely and he consulted his wise men about the problem. One counselor recommended that he divorce Queen Vashti to make an example of her to all the other wives in the kingdom. The king followed his advice and sent Vashti sent away, never to be seen again.

Later, the counselors noticed that the king was very sad about losing Vashti. So, they recommended that a contest be held to select a new queen. This began a search for the loveliest young ladies in the kingdom. All of these radiant beauties were brought to the royal court for the king to choose his favorite.

One of these fair maidens was Esther, a young but wise Jewish girl who lived in the home of her cousin Mordecai. Mordecai was an experienced and honorable man, and he had raised Esther just like his own daughter. Esther was delightful in conversation and conduct, knowing just what to say in every situation.

From the time she arrived at the palace, Esther excelled in everything. The royal court officials liked her immensely and the other maidens admired her stunning beauty.

Esther was so radiant and captivating that the king placed a jeweled, golden crown upon her head and she became his queen. To celebrate the occasion, he invited his officials and servants to a grand feast where he gave generous gifts and refunded large sums of money to his provinces. So it was that Esther began to live in luxury, with many servants, attendants and maids.

Her cousin Mordecai had also risen to be an official in the king's palace. He soon distinguished himself by uncovering a plot against the king. He informed Esther about it and the guards involved were put to death. The details of the incident were recorded in the historical records of the court.

Paradoxically however, the king also appointed a prideful and treacherous man named Haman as prime minister. Haman despised Mordecai because he would not bow to Haman when he passed by. Consumed with hatred, Haman plotted to kill Mordecai and all Jews throughout the kingdom. Haman soon approached the king about "a certain people" whose laws were different and who did not follow his laws (Esther 3:8, KJV). He asked to destroy them and even offered to reimburse the king for any cost involved.

So, the king agreed to Haman's recommendation and allowed him to publish decrees to every province stating that all Jews should be killed, including children. While messengers went out to all government officials, the king and Haman sat down and drank together, unconcerned about the horrible decision. But the whole nation fell into turmoil.

Esther was unaware of any of this until her servants reported that Mordecai was in the street weeping. She was unable to console him and sent one of her attendants to see him. The attendant returned with news of the decrees to destroy the Jews. He also brought a request from Mordecai that Esther plead for mercy from the king.

But Esther reminded Mordecai that those who entered the king's presence without an invitation could be put to death. The only time an exception was made was when the king lifted his golden scepter to receive the visitor.

Mordecai responded bluntly by telling her that if she didn't help, God would find someone who would. And moreover, she and her relatives would die anyway. And *"who can say but that God has brought you into the palace for just such a time as this?"* (Esther 4:14, TLB).

Hearing this, Esther resolved to take action, even if it meant losing her life. She directed Mordecai to gather all the Jews in the land to go without food for three days and pray. She and her maids would do the same. "I will go in to see the king; and if I perish, I perish" (Esther 4:16 TLB).

Following this time of great fasting and prayer, Esther adorned herself in her royal robes and entered the king's inner court. Thankfully, the king lifted his golden scepter, to welcome Esther and spare her life. The queen touched the tip gratefully. Before Esther could make her request, the king passionately promised to give her whatever she wished, "even if it is half of the kingdom." (Esther 5:3). However, Esther did not reveal her intentions at this time; she humbly invited the king and Haman to a banquet.

So the king accepted the invitation and he and Haman hurried off to the feast. While they were enjoying fine wine, the king again reassured Esther that she could have whatever she wanted "even if it is half the kingdom." Always submissive, Esther simply invited him to return the next day with Haman for another banquet. She promised to explain herself then.

After the sumptuous dinner, Haman felt so honored that he went home and boasted to his wife and friends about all the king had done for him and how Esther had invited him to another banquet with the king. But he lamented that all of this good fortune meant nothing to him because Mordecai would not show any respect to him. Haman's wife then suggested that Haman build gallows for Mordecai and hang him in the morning. Haman liked her idea and ordered tall gallows built for Mordecai. But Proverbs 26:27 warns, "If you set a trap for others, you will get caught in it yourself."

That same night, the king was restless and began to read through the official chronicles of the kingdom. He found the account of Mordecai exposing the plot to assassinate him. After reading this, the king decided that Mordecai deserved a reward for his actions.

At that very moment, Haman arrived to talk with him. The king asked Haman how he would reward someone who pleased the king. Supposing that person to be himself, Haman expressed the most lavish and extravagant reward imaginable: that the man wear the king's robe and the king's crown, and ride upon the king's horse, being led through the streets by a nobleman proclaiming his honor. The king agreed and commanded that it be done – *for Mordecai!*

So, while Mordecai rode on horseback through the streets of the city, Haman walked before him holding the horse's bridle. Afterwards, the deeply humiliated Haman returned home sadly, where he explained what had happened. Hearing this, Haman's family and advisors warned him that if Mordecai was Jewish, he would never overcome him. But **before Haman had time to think** about their warning, the king's messengers arrived to escort him to Esther's banquet.

At Esther's sumptuous banquet, they began with wine, as before. And once again, the king pressed Esther, "What is your petition, Queen Esther? What do you wish? Whatever it is, I will give it to you, even if it is half or my kingdom!" (Esther 7:2, TLB). This time Esther was clear about what she wanted: protection of her own life and the lives of her people. The king was utterly aghast that anyone would dare try to harm his queen and demanded to know who this villain was. Esther replied "This wicked Haman is our enemy" (Esther 7:6 TLB).

The king's face grew dark with anger while Haman's face turned pale with fear. The king stormed into the garden and Haman began to plead with Esther for his life. Just as he fell onto the couch where Esther was seated, the king reentered the room. Seeing Haman in this position, he exploded in fury and his guards immediately placed the veil of death over Haman's face.

Then the king's aide informed him that Haman had constructed hanging gallows for Mordecai. So the king commanded that the gallows be used for Haman. God caused a reversal of fortunes as written in Psalm 141:10: "Let the wicked fall into their own nets, but let me escape."

Upon hearing that Mordecai was related to Queen Esther, the king appointed him to fill the position of prime minister. He also gave Haman's home and possessions to Queen Esther, who put Mordecai in charge of the estate.

Once again, Queen Esther approached the king most humbly to petition him to protect all Jews throughout the kingdom. Again the king welcomed her warmly into his presence by raising the scepter toward her.

Although the king regretted his first decree, the laws of the Medes and the Persians could not be cancelled. So the king gave Mordecai authority to publish whatever decree he could devise to counteract the previous edict. Mordecai craftily composed an order that would allow the Jews to band together, kill their aggressors, and take their property. This new letter, combined with the fact that the new Prime Minister was Jewish, took the teeth out of the first decree.

Swift riders carried Mordecai's decrees throughout all 127 provinces of the empire, from Ethiopia to India! Following the great victory, the Jews danced jubilantly, sang joyfully, and gave gifts to one another. Mordecai proclaimed a new annual holiday which is still observed to this day.

On the day which Haman had originally planned for attacking the Jews, no one lifted a finger against them. Because Mordecai was so powerful, even the provincial rulers were quiet.

Then the Jews did away with their enemies throughout the kingdom. And even though Mordecai's decrees granted permission to confiscate property, none was taken.

The Jewish people institutionalized the holiday Purim to remember God's deliverance by placing Esther on the Queen's throne "for such a time as this."

Are you here for a reason and is it time for you to speak up?

Summary and Observations

For this story of heroism to unfold, many events had to occur at just the right time and in just the right order. In His divine sovereignty, God arranged the following:

- Esther needed to be beautiful to be chosen to replace Vashti as queen.
- Esther had to be orphaned for Mordecai to take her in.
- Mordecai had to groom Esther for her future role in the palace.
- Queen Vashti had to refuse the King's invitation to be vanquished.
- Provincial officials had to notice Esther's beauty.
- Mordecai had to instruct Esther not to reveal that she was Jewish. Otherwise, Haman would not have revealed his true feelings.
- The king had to fall in love with her.
- Mordecai had to be chosen as a palace official to uncover the plot against the king's life.
- The king needed to be sleepless the night before Haman came to the outer court. If not, he would not have found the court record of Mordecai's loyal deed.
- The king had to have a sense of fairness to reward Mordecai. "The king's heart is in the

hand of the LORD, as the rivers of water: he turns it whithersoever he will" (Proverbs 21:1).

- Haman had to be blinded by pride and consumed by hatred.
- The king's guards had to appear at Haman's home to take him to the banquet just as he was discussing the problem of Mordecai with his wife and advisors. If not, he would have had time to consider their warning about Mordecai more earnestly.
- Haman's wife had to suggest building the gallows for Mordecai. If not, there would not have been such an ironic and just means of executing Haman at the very moment the king became infuriated.
- The king had to enter the room as Haman was throwing himself at Esther's feet.
- Mordecai had to be an educated and innovative thinker to word the decree that protected the Jews without rescinding the king's previous edict.
- The king had to appoint Mordecai to take Haman's place. Otherwise, lower officials would have been more confident about attacking the Jews.

The overriding theme of this story is God's strategic placement of well-prepared people in the right place at the right time. God knows the end from the beginning and accomplishes his will in the affairs of mankind. "The Most High rules over the kingdoms of the world (Daniel 4:17, NLT)."

Mordecai and Esther worked together from the time that Esther was a child throughout her reign as queen. They understood one another implicitly and communicated frankly. Mordecai's mentoring of Esther had imparted a sense of dignity and served to prepare her for the royal palace.

Mordecai had firsthand knowledge of what was going on in the kingdom, whereas Esther was sheltered from current news. It was only through Mordecai that Esther became aware of the crisis. Likewise, King Xerxes did not know which ethnic group Haman wanted to kill. How easy it is for rulers to lose sight of what is happening among the common people!

As Mordecai had displayed audacity toward Haman, so he did with Esther, despite her new position as queen. Because of his resolute spirit and allegiance to God, Mordecai was able to demand that Esther take action. Esther was the only one with the desire, the daring, and the opportunity to approach the king without an invitation.

Later, because of Esther's proximity to the situation and firsthand knowledge of the events as they occurred, she assumed leadership and called for drastic measures: that the Jewish community pray and fast for three days. Mordecai organized the time of fasting and prayer. Esther and Mordecai showed that they had a willingness to follow and support one another as the situation required. Neither was concerned about being in charge. In reality, God was the leader of this duo and the Jews in the kingdom.

During this time of prayer and fasting, God prepared the king to receive Esther. The king's favor was a crucial part of the plan to topple Haman. These three days were also a time of building Esther's faith for the daring plan ahead. The tremendous power of prayer is evident when one considers the vastness of the king's rule: a kingdom of 127 provinces extending from Ethiopia to India.

Furthermore, Esther demonstrated intrepid skill in building Haman's pride while peaking the king's curiosity about what she wanted. With impeccable timing she lured Haman into her fatal trap, using the bait he most desired – honor (or worship).

In constructing and executing her plan, Esther displayed unusual insight into Haman's character. Due to his hidden lust for the king's throne, Haman was ripe for the picking. His brazen conceit was evidenced by the things he had listed to be given to the man who pleased the king (presuming that man to be himself): he wanted **the king's** clothes, **the king's** horse, and **the king's** crown as well as a nobleman from **the king's** court to proclaim his honor. He actually wanted to take the king's place! This is so reminiscent of Satan's desire to ascend to the throne of heaven! From the Garden of Eden, Satan has tempted people by their desire to be worshipped. "God knows that your eyes will be opened as soon as you eat it, and you will be like God, knowing both good and evil." (Genesis 3:5, NLT). Satan himself fell for this very same temptation: "For you said to yourself, 'I will ascend to heaven and set my throne above God's stars. I will preside on the mountain of the gods far away in the north" (Isaiah

14:13-14, NLT). The temptation to be worshipped is dangerous.

Yet God had plans for Satan and God had plans for Haman. "They hanged Haman on the gallows that he had prepared for Mordecai" (Esther 7:10, KJV).

The story of Mordecai and Esther is about devotion to your kindred people. It is also a story of courage on the part of a man who would not bow to wickedness and a queen who was willing to risk her own life. It is a wonderful example of how God prepares and conditions his people for a lifetime to carry out one monumental task. Although only a young and sheltered lady, Esther was ready to meet her moment of decision, executing an ingenious trap at the precise moment.

But more than anything, it is the story of a skilled Archer drawing a perfect arrow from his quiver, sharpened and polished for one lethal shot, and sending it into the heart of a cruel enemy.

For Such a Time as This

Am I here only to receive the king's kiss
Or wisely placed here for such a time as this?

Will he lift his scepter as I enter his court
Or to his palace guards resort?

I wear the finest apparel, majestic and royal
To be found acceptable, true and loyal.

I and my kinsmen have prayed and fasted
Our earnest prayers have three days lasted.

Now, I'm resigned to trust God's grace
Whether favor or death I come to face

Yet, my palace strong will not protect me
If I am silent about the evil I see.

No, this heroic moment I cannot miss
For I am here for such a time as this.

I approach this king of wealth and might.
Hoping to find favor in his sight

Now, I see his golden scepter raised!
God is strong, and greatly to be praised!

I extend my invitation, a banquet for three
Only the king, my enemy and me.

The table is set along with my plan.
In very few words, I'll accuse this man.

My prideful guest joins the king for wine,
But he will not be staying to dine.

I explain that my people have a cruel enemy,
Willing to pay, our downfall to see.

Yes, a great sum he is willing to lose.
To anyone who destroys the Jews.

My royal husband demands his name.
"The villain and Haman are one in the same."

The king's countenance is dark with rage.
He paces angrily like a lion in a cage.

His command goes out with royal powers.
Pale and helpless, Haman cowers.

Soon, he hangs from the gallows he built.
Designed for Mordecai, a man with no guilt.

A wiser king reverses Haman's decrees.
He constrains the ruthless, but the Jews he frees.

Our victory is complete, our enemies defeated
And next to the king, Mordecai is seated!

Each year we will celebrate, and never miss
When I was brought to the kingdom *for such a
time as this!*

Mordecai and Esther

A Study in Risk-Taking

QUESTIONS TO CONSIDER

1) **God placed Queen Esther in her influential royal position at a critical time.**

   a) Is it possible that you were brought here to serve a specific role?
   b) What might your specific role be?
   c) Do you like to blend in or stand out in a group? Is there a time for both?

2) **Esther needed social skills and wisdom in the royal palace.**

   a) What skills and strengths would past coworkers say you have?
   b) What skills are most evident?
   c) What areas would you like to improve upon?
   d) Do you think your coworkers will appreciate your talents?

3) **The Medo-Persian King Xerxes rewarded Mordecai for his loyalty.**

   a) Do you anticipate that your efforts will be rewarded?

b) What other expectations do you have?

c) Is anything you do for God ever wasted? "Nothing you do for the Lord is ever useless" (1 Corinthians 15:58, TLB).

4) The king was very approachable and accessible. In fact, he became impatient when she did not voice her request at first.

a) Is timing important in presenting your concerns to those in authority?

b) How formal should your relationship be with those higher in the organization?

c) Is there an appropriate time to approach leaders?

d) When leaders are busy with important matters, is it a good time to see them?

e) When leaders are angry, is it a good time to approach them?

f) Is God impatient for you to ask Him for blessings? "Until now you have not asked for anything in my name. Ask and you will receive, and your joy will be complete" (John 16:24, NIV)

5) Many events had to happen at the right time for Esther to assume the throne.

a) Can you think of five things that had to occur in order for you to be here?

b) Which of these did you influence?

c) Which were beyond your control?

6) Esther and Mordecai worked together closely, and at times, exchanged leadership roles depending on who had the latest and most accurate information.

a) In your group, what situations might arise which would necessitate rotating leadership or coordination responsibilities?

b) Are you willing to "step up" and lead if you are the best equipped for the task?

c) What might happen if you do not lead when needed?

d) Are you willing to risk your personal welfare to defend someone in danger?

e) Are you will to support and follow a former coworker who may be chosen to lead?

f) Can you maintain a good attitude when supporting a former peer who has been promoted?

7) One of the endeavors that Esther and Mordecai coordinated was corporate prayer.

a) Can you name five people who would be willing to pray for you if asked?

b) King Xerxes was anxious to hear Esther's requests. Is it hard to get God's attention?

Mordecai and Esther

A Study in Risk-Taking

GROUP DISCUSSION QUESTIONS AND ACTIVITIES

"The Ideal Leader" (Class Discussion)

Ask each class member to tell one characteristic of a leader that they most appreciate. List the attributes on the board.

Are these most of the attributes linked to technical expertise or character qualities?

Discuss what makes a good leader.

Objective: To formulate a profile of a great leader.

"High Expectations" (Small Group Interaction)

Each group formulates a list of their top ten expectations and ranks their importance from one to ten.

A representative shares the group's list and create a master list on the board.

Create a master list of 10 expectations, prioritized from most important to least important.

Objective: To clarify goals and begin to form a corporate culture by identifying shared values.

To Be or Not to Be

Do you think Esther considered remaining silent about the plight of the Jews?

What amount of courage did it take for Esther to approach the king?

Would Queen Esther benefit by keeping quiet about the danger to her people?

Institutionalizing Success

This story did not stop with Mordecai's decree to protect the Jews. Another declaration by Mordecai created the annual holiday, Purim, which Jews still observe throughout the world today.

Successful teams often achieve great things. However, they often fail to record the methods and strategies that brought success. Teams disperse without leaving a written record of the steps taken to accomplish their objective.

When your team achieves its goals, it is important to review and document how you did it; including the decisions, the risks, and the tactics. Make successful methods part of your standard operating procedures. It is critical to formalized successful procedures.

It is also critical to celebrate success to build it into your corporate culture. This defines who you are and what traits your team prizes.

It creates a tradition of winning and provides encouragement for future challenges.

Why do Americans celebrate the 4th of July?

Why do couples celebrate wedding anniversaries?

What is the purpose of looking back on great accomplishments?

How does this prepare your team for the future?

How many times has God intervened in your life?

When is the best time to approach a person in authority?

When is a bad time to approach a powerful individual?

What are the dangers of barging into someone's office at the wrong time?

Caught in his own trap

How many times have you seen evil plots boomerang on someone?

CHAPTER 8

NEHEMIAH AND COMPANY

A Study in Passion and Persistence

Nehemiah's name means "God's compassion." Certainly, God put a burning love for Jerusalem in Nehemiah's heart and Nehemiah followed his passion – at any cost. The story of this team is that a passionate and godly leader succeeds against all odds. Nehemiah's legacy is his fire, fueled by the power of God.

Nehemiah's job was to keep his own spirits up. As a member of the Persian royal court, he had personal access to the king – and cheerfulness was mandatory. However, when Nehemiah discovered that his beloved Jerusalem had fallen into disrepair, his bright expression turned to tears and his vibrant demeanor vanished. After sitting down and weeping, Nehemiah refused food for several days, passionately crying out to God from a broken heart.

Nehemiah's prayer reveals a knowledge of the character and power of God. Knowing that God inhabits the praises of his people, Nehemiah began by honoring the "Lord God of heaven, the great and terrible God" (Nehemiah 1:5, KJV). Then, convinced that God is always dependable, Nehemiah reminded him of his commandments to Moses. God's promise to accept his children when they turn from their sin was recited: "But if you return to me and obey my laws, even though you are exiled to the farthest corners of the universe, I will bring you back to Jerusalem" (Nehemiah 1:9 TLB). Finally, he knew that "the king's heart is in the hand of the Lord" (Proverbs 21:1). Nehemiah asked God to give him favor from the king of Persia (Nehemiah 1:11, KJV).

Four months later, as Nehemiah was carrying out his customary duties, the king noticed something unusual in his excellent attendant: sadness. The questioned him about this, "Why is your countenance sad, seeing you are not sick? This is nothing else but sorrow of heart" (Nehemiah 2:2, KJV). Shaken badly by the king's observation, Nehemiah realized that this was the very moment for which he had been praying. So he explained that Jerusalem, the city of his fathers, was in ruin. The king responded, "For what do you make request?" (Nehemiah 2:4, KJV). Nehemiah immediately called on God, "With a quick prayer to the God of heaven, I replied ... send me to Judah to rebuild the city" (Nehemiah 2:5 TLB). "So it *pleased* the king to send me." Nehemiah, encouraged by the king's approval, and having already planned the project, added a request for logistical support. It is interesting that Nehemiah did not proceed to this request until after he had first obtained the king's endorsement of the project.

This project would require emotional investment, self-defense, and hard work. Even though Nehemiah had become accustomed the palace, none of these challenges deterred him.

Nehemiah knew, in vivid detail, what Jerusalem should look like. The memories of its bustling streets and beautiful gardens were still very clear in his mind, and he wanted to restore Jerusalem to prominence. But the dilapidated condition of the great city made it clear that no one else shared this vision.

The apathy and blindness of his countrymen explains why Nehemiah did not announce his intentions earlier. Human nature requires a crisis before taking drastic action. So, Nehemiah traveled to Jerusalem and quietly surveyed the ruins, gaining firsthand knowledge of the situation. Stirred by what he saw, Nehemiah met with key citizens, face-to-face, to express his disgust about the wasted city and the reproach it had brought upon all of them. He then addressed their fears by assuring them that he had the king's support as well as God's blessing. Confronted by the shame all around them and inspired by Nehemiah's resolve, everyone committed to the task.

Their historic work reveals a number of principles about great undertakings.

Clarify the Enemy: Two scoffers, Sanballat and Tobiah, immediately accused Nehemiah of rebelling against the king. Whenever you do something significant, expect criticism. Nehemiah's response was blunt: "The God of heaven will help us, and we, his servants, will rebuild this wall; but you may have no part in this affair" (Nehemiah 2:20 TLB). He drew a clear distinction between the two camps: those who were for him, and those who were against him. In a misty and shadowy world, it is important to name the enemy, to bring him out into the open. Also notice that Nehemiah placed his confidence in God's power, not his own.

Acknowledge God: Although the priests made up a small part of the population, they were the first to rebuild the wall. What they lacked in building expertise, they made up in zeal, not only rebuilding the sheep gate, but hanging its doors as well. And this small minority dedicated the accomplishment to God (Nehemiah 3:1). Honoring God with their initial success was an important "first fruits" offering. The priests knew never to take credit for what God was doing, lest he remove his blessing.

Job Enlargement Motivates: In Nehemiah 3:3, one crew built the fish gate from start to finish, including making the parts. Having responsibility for the whole structure leaves no room for room for finger-pointing about poor suppliers or unskilled workers.

AUTHORITY + RESPONSIBILITY = ACCOUNTABILITY

There is also a psychological benefit that comes from completing an entire assignment. Such satisfaction is not experienced by simply doing a small repetitive task for many other ongoing projects. Starting a job is thrilling, but there is nothing like finishing.

Succeed Despite a Lack of Supervision: In Nehemiah 3:5, we see that it is possible to succeed even under weak management. Further down the wall, the men of Tekoa worked, but with poor leadership. Nehemiah makes it a point to record this: "Their leaders were lazy and didn't help" (Nehemiah 3:5 TLB). What a horrible way to be remembered in doing God's work! Freeloading supervisors will be noticed.

Resumes Do Not Reflect Desire: The book of Nehemiah records that much of the work was done by those who were untrained in construction. Many goldsmiths, politicians, priests, and one perfume maker, took up carpentry and masonry. Zeal and passion more than compensated for a lack of experience.

Cooperation of Church and State: Even mayors of various parts of Jerusalem worked with stone and mortar. Not too far away, priests and temple attendants were building the wall. The cooperation between politicians and clergy proves that church and state can work together. Does it make sense to argue about jurisdiction when enemies are trying to destroy your homeland?

Vested Interest Assures Quality: Nehemiah directed each priest to construct the portion of the wall near his own house. This, of course, provided the priests a true incentive to do a good job. Responsibility is reinforced when you know that your own family's wellbeing depends on the quality of your work.

We also see this principle applied after the wall is finished. Guards were required to be residents of Jerusalem (Nehemiah 3:3). Homeowners were required to guard the section of the wall next to their own homes (Nehemiah 3:4).

Let God Deal with the Enemy: As Nehemiah and company made progress, criticism intensified. The outraged enemy Sanballat increased his mockery and scoffing. However, he unwittingly helped Nehemiah when he assailed the religion of the Jews. Within hearing range of the builders, Sanballat mocked: "Will they sacrifice?" (Nehemiah 4:2, KJV). This gave Nehemiah a talking point with God. Rather than neglecting his work to attack Sanballat, Nehemiah brought the matter to God: "They have provoked you to anger before the builders" (Nehemiah 4:5, KJV). As soon as Nehemiah asked God to become the Sovereign Team Leader over the work, results occurred. The very next verse tells us that the wall was connected all the way around the city.

Persistent Enemies Require Persistent Prayer: Nehemiah 4:7-9 tells us that Sanballat, and his henchmen were furious about the on-going success of the project. They planned a military attack accompanied by riots. Again, Nehemiah turned to God. Furthermore, he did his best to protect his interests, guarding the city "**day and night.**" Nehemiah persisted because he knew that Jerusalem was his homeland and that Sanballat was a mere trespasser.

Internal Trouble May Occur at the Worst Time: Just when Nehemiah needed his subordinate leaders to be strong, some of them began to complain. While complaining is not a trait you want in your key officers, even good workers can get tired. Right away, Nehemiah called the leaders and people together to encourage them. He didn't talk about his talents, his fighting ability, or his wisdom. Instead, he encouraged them to "remember the Lord, which is great and terrible, and fight for your brethren, your sons, and your daughters, your wives, and your houses" (Nehemiah 4:14, KJV). He could have promised them lofty positions, individual awards, or money. But he knew what his brethren counted precious: faith, family, and homes. Nehemiah's brilliance was in keeping things on track, despite the enemy's efforts to derail his efforts. He was able to keep hope alive by refreshing the vision of a safe and secure homeland. Once the work crews refocused on God, they stopped bickering and were able to see that their problems were really not very big in comparison to God's strength.

It is wise to meet with subordinate leaders prior to the start of a major project. They need to set the example for the workforce by maintaining a positive attitude.

Readiness without Reliance: Nehemiah's workers kept their swords within reach and Nehemiah kept his trumpeter at his side, ready to sound the alarm. Military response tactics were rehearsed and half of the workforce stayed on guard. Work continued from sunrise to sunset, with no one even taking time to change clothes. Despite his wholehearted effort, Nehemiah never trusted in his own ability to succeed. "Our God shall fight for us" (Nehemiah 5:19, KJV).

Fierce Anger is Appropriate for Unacceptable Conduct. Some of the wealthier Jews were charging their needy brethren excessively on their debts. Nehemiah records that he became "very angry" (Nehemiah 5:6, KJV) and put an end to this practice.

Take Time to Think Before Acting: Nehemiah demonstrated reason and calm just at the time when others would have lost control. Before taking action, Nehemiah pondered the problem and what to do. "*after thinking about it* I spoke out against these rich government officials" (Nehemiah 5:7 TLB).

Take Action to Restore Justice: "Then I called a public trial to deal with them" (Nehemiah 5:7 TLB). This was a serious matter that required a serious response. Nehemiah achieved resolution in a fair and just way and secured the solemn promise of the offenders to abide by the decision. Once again, we see Nehemiah guiding affairs on a continuous basis to maintain order. Is it any wonder they followed a leader who put their wellbeing ahead of his own?

Demonstrate Unselfishness: Nehemiah did not accept a salary because he knew it would be a burden on the workers. He complained to no one, although he did ask God to reward him in verse 5:19: "Think upon me, my God, for good, according to all that I have done for this people." It is clear that Nehemiah was willing to sacrifice for the good of his people. Nehemiah knew that God, not man, was his ultimate Provider.

Don't be Intimidated: As the project neared completion, Nehemiah's enemies stepped up their threats. They tried to draw him away from work to kill him, but Nehemiah refused to be distracted. "I am doing a great work! Why should I stop to come and visit with you?" (Nehemiah 6:3 TLB). Four more times they sent requests, including an accusation that Nehemiah was subverting the king's authority. Nehemiah continued his successful pattern of rebuke and prayer. Finally, Tobiah and Sanballat hired another Jew to persuade Nehemiah to lock himself in the Temple, which would have given them cause for accusation, since Nehemiah was not a priest. Nehemiah's reply? "Should I, the governor, run away from danger?" (Nehemiah 6:11 TLB).

Don't Waste Time. Nehemiah and his fellow countrymen completed the Jerusalem wall in only 52 days. They worked with a <u>sense of urgency</u>.

There is No Success Without a Successor. Following completion of the wall, Nehemiah gave responsibility for governing to his brother Hanani and to the fortress commander, Hananiah. He also left them with instructions about security procedures. Nehemiah not only appointed them, he told them **how** to succeed.

Thank God in Joyful Celebration. Nehemiah assembled all the people and Ezra the priest to worship the Lord. "Go your way, eat the fat, and drink the sweet, and send portions unto them for whom nothing is prepared: for this day is holy unto our Lord: neither be sorry; for the joy of the Lord is your strength." (Nehemiah 8:10, KJV).

Remember Why God Gave You Success. "So, the people went away to eat a festive meal and to send presents; it was a time of great and joyful celebration *because they could hear and understand God's words* (Nehemiah 8:12 TLB). Always remember why God brings us out of the ruins: *SO THAT WE CAN WORSHIP HIM*.

Nehemiah and Company: A Study in Passion
QUESTIONS TO CONSIDER

There are three critical elements for success in great achievements:

- **PASSION**
- **PRAYER**
- **PERSISTENCE**

The first element, passion, is the combustible fuel for the other two elements: prayer and persistence. You may have made the decision to pursue this course of action because you were sick of your current situation. Like Nehemiah, you may have hit you emotional "bottom." Although he had comfortable surroundings and a good income, his heart yearned for something more noble, more admirable. Nehemiah liked a challenge.

1. **Consider Nehemiah's reaction when he first learned of the dilapidated condition of his hometown of Jerusalem: (Nehemiah 1: 4): "<u>And it came to pass, when I heard these words, that I sat down and wept, and mourned certain days, and fasted, and prayed before the God of heaven.</u>"**

a. What do Nehemiah's reactions reveal about his feelings for Jerusalem?
b. To whom did Nehemiah turn first?

2. **In its glorious past, Jerusalem had been a source of pride and joy to Nehemiah and his people. The capital city had represented faith, culture, industry, and strength. Because of neglect, Jerusalem had been reduced to shambles and had become an eye sore. Have you seen situations like this?**

a. Can you name a time that you were excluded from an opportunity due to your own lack of effort?
   - At work?
   - In a social setting?
   - In a financial transaction?
b. Was your self-esteem affected? How so?
c. With a little more effort and diligence, what could you achieve?
   - Professionally?
   - Socially?
   - Financially?

3. **In the first chapter, just after collapsing in sorrow, Nehemiah prayed to God.**

a. Why did Nehemiah pray before approaching the king for help?
b. Does this show that Nehemiah intends to **take action** about his passion?

4. **Later in the book, Nehemiah says that God gave him the passion to complete the rebuilding. (Nehemiah 2:12) "And I arose in the night, I and some few men with me; neither told I any man** *what my God had put in my heart to do* **at Jerusalem."**

   a. Is it possible that **God Himself** has put a desire in **your** heart?
   b. Does God want to do something through you?
   c. Are you comfortable with yielding to God's plans for you?
   d. Is completing a project **its own reward**, regardless of criticism?
   e. Do you believe that "getting there is half the fun"?
   f. Do we harvest what we plant?

5. **The priests were the first team to rebuild their portion of the wall. The first thing they did was dedicate their work to God, giving him credit for its completion. There is a promise in Proverbs 3:9-10 for those who practice this: Honor the Lord with your substance, and with the first fruits of all your increase: So shall your barns be filled with plenty, and your presses shall burst out with new wine.**

   a. How can you acknowledge God after your first success?
   b. What may happen if you take all the credit for your achievements? 1 Peter 5:5: "God resists

the proud." Anything that does not result in praise turns to pride.

6. **Although Nehemiah had enemies and discouraged workers, he was not discouraged or intimidated.**

   a. How did Nehemiah deal with persistent enemies?
   b. Did he have a different practice for each challenge?
   c. How did he maintain his courage and faith?
   d. How do you obtain emotional support? "Casting all your care upon him; for he cares for you." (1 Peter 5:7)

7. **The Bible tells us that Nehemiah fed over 150 people every day. Yet, Nehemiah did not tax the workers, so he must have paid for this himself.**

   a. What does this reveal about Nehemiah's emotional commitment?

8. **Nehemiah maintained his passion from beginning to end. This was evident by the heated words he had with people who were taking advantage of others.**

   a. Do you believe "**Open rebuke is better than secret love**" (Proverbs 27:5).
   b. Is there a good way to handle interpersonal conflict and disagreement? It is best to avoid

conflict if possible. "Avoiding a fight is a mark of honor; only fools insist on quarreling" (Proverbs 20:3, NLT).

c. In Matthew 18:15-17, Jesus gave three steps for conflict resolution:
    i.   Discuss the problem one-on-one.
    ii. If that does not work, take two or three people with you.
    iii. If that does not work, bring the matter before the whole group.

Nehemiah and Company: A Study in Passion

DISCUSSION QUESTIONS AND ACTIVITIES

Doing Whatever it Takes

Have you ever observed anyone like Nehemiah who had a burning desire to achieve a project that was so great that he or she would make any sacrifice for it?

Was the attitude contagious?

Objective: To reinforce the lessons of Nehemiah with contemporary examples.

Different Strokes for Different Folks

Rebuilding the walls of Jerusalem required constant effort and personal sacrifice.

Who or what would motivate **you** to undertake such a project?

Objective: To demonstrate that different people have different motivations.

You can make a good man able, but you can't make an able man good.

In this modern age of job specialization, can you work outside of your field and still be successful? What situations might necessitate doing work outside your training and education?

Have you ever been in a situation where you found a compressed learning curve? Was it stressful, exhilarating, or both? Did you discover new abilities and talents?

Objective: To recognize that team members will be "stretching" their elastic minds in new and different ways of thinking.

Small Group Interaction: "Pick Your Leader"

In small groups, identify ten current leaders you would gladly follow in a crisis. Prioritize them from one to ten with the most capable being number one.

Reconvene so that each small group can share their list.

Write them on the board and have the class vote for the top five.

Objective: To recognize the value of various personality traits to the team's success.

Small Group Interaction: "High Expectations"

In small groups, list 10 expectations of the group about performance.

Invite each member to sign the list agreeing to abide by it.

Objectives:
To inform people of what is expected of them.
To prevent conflicts.
To gain an appreciation for good attitudes.
To obtain "buy in" by all members.

Small Group Interaction: "Breaking Up the Cat Fight"

In small groups, document a procedure for conflict resolution.

The system should include steps and timeframes to successfully deal with problems such as tardiness and poor work.

Reconvene and share their steps.

Discuss refinements based on the input of other groups.

Objective: To become aware that conflicts may arise and that there are good ways to deal with them.

Small Group Interaction: "Road Show"

In small groups, document the steps in preparing and executing a successful group presentation. At a minimum, the procedure should address:

- a devotional and prayer
- technology
- expeditious means of communicating information to one another
- meeting places and times
- assignment of duties and due dates
- rehearsals
- presentation techniques
- critique and continual improvement

Reconvene and share their group presentation process.

Discuss to identify any enhancements that can be made.

Objective: To develop a process/methodology for group presentations.

CHAPTER 9

THE WISE MEN

A Study in Taking Action

And unto man he said, Behold, the fear of the Lord, that is wisdom; and *to depart from evil* is understanding. Job 28:28

The desert's warm, dry, uneven breeze pressed against his weathered turban. His loose, layered robe flapped against his camel's side; another day plodding through the hot, soft sand. Despite riding since early morning, an aching back, and a parched tongue, he and his companions pushed on, sorely wanting to squeeze one last mile before the sun set behind the wind-swept dunes. Neither the blazing sun nor hard hours in the saddle had diminished their passion. "Forge on. Forge on," they mulled.

This band of determined friends had carefully planned this arduous trip. Their able-bodied servants had loaded additional camels with food, clothing and supplies. Their guards were heavily armed and watchful for any suspicious movement. Their cargo was especially valuable; gold, frankincense, and myrrh. These travelers had packed everything needed for such a long journey: everything except a map.

These learned travelers followed a celestial guide: the prophesied star proclaiming the King of the Jews. They had recognized the supernatural beacon as the fulfillment of ancient scripture. "A Star shall come out of Jacob; A Scepter shall rise out of Israel." Risking their lives and fortunes, they had embarked on the greatest adventure in the history of mankind: the quest to find the Savior! On and on they journeyed, through scorching days and shivering nights. Though their bodies were sore, there was excitement and anticipation in their eyes as they pressed on.

The star led them to Israel where they went to King Herod's court in Jerusalem. When they asked where the "King of the Jews" would be born, the governor called for the Jewish scholars who informed him that the Messiah would be born in Bethlehem. The sly Herod feigned interest in worshipping the new Savior and told the wise men to find the child and return with news of his whereabouts. However, he was gravely concerned about the possibility of another king in his domain. Moreover, because of Herod's temper, everyone in Jerusalem was worried that there would be trouble.

When the wise men left Herod's palace, the star appeared to them again. They followed it directly to the house where Jesus, Mary and Joseph were. With reverence, fear and wonder, they entered the house and fell down to worship the young child. They also presented gold, frankincense, and myrrh to him.

Later, while they were sleeping, God warned them not to return to Herod. They slipped quietly into the night and returned to their own country by a different route.

This fascinating story reveals the different attitudes of man toward God. What a stark contrast between the foreigners' wise, passionate quest to see Jesus and the Israelites' disregard for their own Messiah! The scribes and the Pharisees knew the prophesied birthplace of the Messiah, but never took a single step toward nearby Bethlehem!

This had been a long-standing fault in the Israel's history. Foreigners had often received the blessings that God had intended for His own people. In the days of Elijah, God sent the prophet to sustain the widow of Sarepta, a foreigner, while many Jews suffered throughout the drought (1 Kings 17, KJV). In the time of Elisha, the leper Syrian general Naaman humbled himself and was healed, while many in Israel remained diseased (2 Kings 5). And even later during the ministry of Jesus, a Roman military officer approached the Lord for a miracle and impressed him so much that "he marveled, and said to them that followed, 'Truly I say unto you, *I have not found so great faith, no, not in Israel.*'" (Matthew 8:10, KJV).

Such blindness and apathy angered God. Although He had sent many prophets to prepare Israel to receive their Savior, the Jews were not expecting him. For their oversight, God destroyed Jerusalem in 70 A.D. at the hands of the Roman army.

Contrast Israel's disregard with the foreign visitors' zeal. Even though they did not have Micah's prophesy about the Lord's birth city Bethlehem, the wise men fulfilled Isaiah's ancient prophecy that "they shall bring gold and incense; and they shall show forth the praises of the Lord" (Isaiah 60:6). They acted on what knowledge they had.

The Bible does not state the number or nationality of the wise men. Wisdom is not restricted to a certain race or ethnic group. "*Wisdom shouts in the streets for a hearing. She calls out to the crowds along Main Street, and to the judges in their courts, and to everyone in all the land.*" (Proverbs 1:20, 21, TLB). God offers wisdom to all who seek him.

The wise men received more detailed guidance only after they acted on what they knew. They may have chosen to go to Jerusalem because of its historic prominence. When they arrived, they were not too proud to ask questions. The more knowledge they used, the more they acquired. Jesus taught, "To those who listen to my teaching, more understanding will be given, and they will have an abundance of knowledge (Matthew 13:12, TLB).

Their objective was fixed, but their plans were flexible. The wise men were committed to finding and worshipping Jesus. Once they fulfilled their purpose, God warned them not to return home the same way they had come. So, they changed their route. "The wise are cautious and avoid danger." (Proverbs 14:16, TLB)

The wise men gave us an example of how to worship. They rejoiced vigorously. They fell down and worshipped him. They presented gifts to Him. (Matthew 2: 9-11). These men determined that the wisest thing to do was to find Jesus and worship him. "Oh that men would praise the LORD" (Psalm 107:31, KJV).

The wise travel together. The Bible does not mention any unlearned followers in this group. There were no weak links in this chain. This was an important expedition and there were none in the group who might jeopardize its success. "He that walks with wise men shall be wise: but a companion of fools shall be destroyed." (Proverbs 13:20, KJV)

These men seized the opportunity to worship the Lord. There would never be another incarnation. They did not know if their own health or circumstances would permit them to visit the King later in life. Nor did they know when the King of the Jews would be accessible again. They did know one thing: this was a marvelous opportunity to see and worship the Lord. They seized the opportunity. They answered the call of Wisdom: "I love them that love me; and those that seek me early shall find me" (Proverbs 8: 17).

The wise men had a sense of the greatness of this event. To make the long journey from the east, the wise men had to leave what they were doing, invest time and money in preparation, and embark upon the unknown. They chose to abandon the hustle and bustle of daily life and pursue this once-in-eternity opportunity, even if it cost them everything. Furthermore, they had prepared themselves, emotionally and materially, to respond to the event. "Do not let yourself become tied up in worldly affairs, for then you cannot satisfy the one who has enlisted you" (2 Timothy 2:4, TLB). Wisdom all starts with a choice. "How can men be wise? The only way to begin is by reverence for God. For growth in wisdom comes from obeying his laws" (Psalm 111:10, TLB).

Later in the Bible, there are other exemplary men and women who left their earthly work responsibilities for a divine mission.

The apostles, Peter and Andrew. "As Jesus was walking by Lake Galilee, he saw two brothers, Simon (called Peter) and Simon's brother Andrew. These brothers were fishermen, and they were fishing in the lake with a net. Jesus said to them, "Come, follow me, and I will make you a different kind of fishermen. You will bring in people, not fish." Simon and Andrew immediately left their nets and followed him. (Matthew 4:18-19, ERV)

- *The apostles James and John*. "He called to them to come too. At once they stopped their work and, leaving their father behind, went with him. (Matthew 4:21-22, TLB). Great opportunities may come early in life, while you are energetic and fit. Are you prepared to respond when called?
- **Mary, the sister of Martha, neglected house guests to hear Jesus:** "But one thing is needful: and *Mary has chosen that good part*, which shall not be taken away from her." (Luke 10: 42, KJV)

- ***Mary seized the chance to honor the Lord extravagantly.*** "Mary brought in a pint¹ of expensive perfume made of pure nard. She poured the perfume on Jesus' feet. Then she wiped his feet with her hair. And the sweet smell from the perfume filled the whole house... Jesus answered, 'Don't stop her. It was right for her to save this perfume for today—the day for me to be prepared for burial. You will always have those who are poor with you. But you will not always have me'" (John 12:3, 7-8 ERV). When you get the chance to serve God, seize the opportunity!

What application do the wise men give us? The wise men gave us a model of anticipation regarding the return of the Lord. "You also must be ready all the time, for the Son of Man will come when least expected." (Luke 12:40, TLB)

We can respond or not. You know very well that the Lord is returning one day. Are you prepared? The doers of the Word will be blessed, not the hearers only. "But when you look into God's perfect law that sets people free, pay attention to it. If you do what it says, you will have God's blessing." (JAMES 1:25, ERV).

Proverbs 3:13
Happy is the man that finds wisdom, and the man that gets understanding.

The Wise Men STEP-BY-STEP		
ACTION	**REASON**	**BIBLICAL SUPPORT**
They left their homes in the East.	For true riches: to honor God. "For everything comes from him and exists by his power and is intended for his glory. All glory to him forever! Amen." (Romans 11:36, NLT)	"Wisdom is the main pursuit." (Proverbs 17:24, TLB) "How much better is wisdom than gold, and understanding than silver!" (Proverbs 16:16)
They traveled together.	"Though one may be overpowered, two can defend themselves. A cord of three strands is not quickly broken." (Ecclesiastes 4:12, NIV)	"Be with wise men and become wise." (Proverbs 13:20, TLB)
They came from the east to Jerusalem. (Matt 2:1-2)	To find Jesus and worship him. (Matthew 2:2, NKJV)	"Have two goals: wisdom – that is, knowing and doing right – and common sense." (Pr. 3:21)
They asked "Where is He who has been born King of the Jews? (Matthew 2:2)	They were willing to ask directions. "A wise man is hungry for truth." (Proverbs 15:14, TLB)	"A wise man listens to others." (Proverbs12:15, TLB)

ACTION	REASON	BIBLICAL SUPPORT
They had followed His star in the East. (Matthew 2:2)	They had been looking for divine guidance. It came obviously and clearly in the form of a brilliant star.	"Wisdom shouts" (Prov 1:20) "Come here and listen to me! Turn at my rebuke; Surely I will pour out my spirit on you; I will make my words known to you." (Proverbs 1:23)
They had come to worship Him. (Matthew 2:2)	Due to the God's history with the Jews, the wise men must have viewed their king as divine.	Exodus from Egypt. The giving of the Ten Commandments. (Exodus 20).
They met with King Herod privately. They told Herod when the star had appeared to them. (Matthew 2:7) He asked them to find Jesus and reveal his location. (Matt. 2:9)	King Herod called them. (Matthew 2:7, NKJV))	'He sent them to Bethlehem and said, "Go and search carefully for the child. As soon as you find him, report to me, so that I too may go and worship him."' (Matt 2:8 NIV)

ACTION	REASON	BIBLICAL SUPPORT
They left Herod and saw the star. They rejoiced with exceedingly great joy. (Matthew 2:10)	In your presence *is* fullness of joy (Psalm 16:11, KJV)	"For wisdom and truth will enter the very center of your being, filling your life with joy." (Proverbs 2:10)
They followed the star to the house where Jesus, Mary, and Joseph were. (Matthew 2:11)	They were persistent. "Determination to be wise is the first step toward becoming wise!" (Proverbs 4:7, TLB)	"The path of those who live right is like the early morning light. It gets brighter and brighter until the full light of day." (Proverbs 4:18 ERV)
They fell down and worshipped him. (Matthew 2:11)	Submit to God's royal son, or he will become angry, and you will be destroyed in the midst of all your activities. (Psalm 2:12, NLT)	Oh come, let us worship and bow down; let us kneel before the LORD, our Maker! (Psalm 95:6, ESV)
They gave Jesus gold, frankincense, and myrrh. (Matthew 2:11)	The eastern kings of Sheba and Seba will bring him gifts. (Ps. 72:10, NLT)	Long live the king! May the gold of Sheba be given to him. (Psalm 72:15, NLT)

ACTION	REASON	BIBLICAL SUPPORT
God warned them in a dream that they should not return to Herod. So, they left the country without going back through Jerusalem. (Matthew 2:12)	Herod was a violent, evil person. Because he did not want any competition, he killed all the young boys, age two and under, in Bethlehem. "Then Herod, when he saw that he was deceived by the wise men, was exceedingly angry; and he sent forth and put to death all the male children who were in Bethlehem and in all its districts, from two years old and under, according to the time which he had determined from the wise men." (Matthew 2:16 NKJV)	"The wise man looks ahead." (Pr. 14:8, TLB) "A wise man is cautious and avoids danger." (Proverbs 14:16, TLB) "The anger of the king is a messenger of death and a wise man will appease it." (Proverbs 14:16, TLB) "But whoever walks wisely will be delivered." (Proverbs 28:26 NKJV)

Wisdom and Wise Men

Wisdom Defined.

Behold, the fear of the Lord, that *is* wisdom; And to depart from evil *is* understanding. (Job 28:28)

What is the Difference Between God's Wisdom and Man's Wisdom?

MAN'S "WISDOM"

So what about these wise men, these scholars, these brilliant debaters of this world's great affairs? God has made them all look foolish and shown their wisdom to be useless nonsense.
(1 Corinthians 1:20, NLT)

The wisdom of this world is foolishness with God.
(1 Corinthians 3:19, KJV)

For the foolishness of God is wiser than human wisdom, and the weakness of God is stronger than human strength. (1 Corinthians 1:25, NIV)

For jealousy and selfishness are not God's kind of wisdom. Such things are earthly, unspiritual, inspired by the devil. (James 3:15, TLB)

<u>**GOD's WISDOM**</u>:

But the wisdom that comes from heaven is first of all pure and full of quiet gentleness. Then it is peace-loving and courteous. It allows discussion and is willing to yield to others; it is full of mercy and good deeds. It is wholehearted and straightforward and sincere. (James 3:17, TLB)

Don't copy the behavior and customs of this world, but be a new and different person with a fresh newness in all you do and think. Then you will learn from your own experience how **his ways** will really satisfy you. (Romans 12:2, TLB)

The Source of Wisdom

For the LORD gives wisdom; from His mouth come knowledge and understanding. He stores up sound wisdom for the upright. (Proverbs 2:6, BLB)

Every word of God *is* pure. (Proverbs 30:5, KJV)

QUESTIONS TO CONSIDER

The Bible is silent about what country the wise men came from.

Is wisdom limited to a certain geographical area?

Do all people have the same opportunity to become wise?

First Hand Experience

Why did the wise men go to Israel themselves as opposed to sending an emissary?

When was the last time you dropped everything to experience something extraordinary?

I myself will see him with my own eyes—I, and not another. How my heart yearns within me!
(Job 19:27, NIV)

Questions to Ask Ourselves:

Have I evaluated a goal, planned my next journey, and counted the costs?

Do I enjoy learning new things?

Is it better to discover something myself or to have someone tell me about it?

Preparation is the secret of success.

Do you know exactly how long the journey will take?
Do you think the wise men built in time and money for unexpected delays?
Do you think the wise men enjoyed the journey?
Did the wise men need faith to complete their work?
Did the wise men need faith to return safely to their own country?

Getting there is half the fun.

When I am on a long, arduous journey, does it help to think about the destination?
Why did the wise men travel together?
What interests did they share?
What practices and activities did they share?
Do you have reliable, wise companions on the journey?
A chain is only as strong as its weakest link.
A team is only as strong as its weakest member.

The wise men interrupted their occupational work to travel to Israel.

Am I willing to be interrupted to pursue a once in a lifetime experience?
Am I willing to spend time, effort and money to find "true riches?"
Is Wisdom my top priority?

New Paradigms

The wise men were probably surprised that Jesus was not in a palace. Their long-held ideas about how a royal court should look vanished. Yet, they now had a new and fresh perspective about the reign of this new King and his purpose on earth.

- Do you have any preconceived notions about your upcoming experience?
- Are you open to change?

Objective: To suggest that your perspectives may change as you go forward.

When they found the Lord and presented gifts to him, do you think they remembered the hardships of their travel?

Finishing is better than starting. (Ecclesiastes 7:8, TLB)

When a woman is giving birth, she has sorrow because her hour has come, but when she has delivered the baby, she no longer remembers the anguish, for joy that a human being has been born into the world. (John 16:21, ESV)

Don't miss the boat!

When the wise men finally returned to their own country, do you think they found others who regretted not going with them?

They will crush you into the ground, and your children with you. Your enemies will not leave a single stone in place, because you did not recognize it when God visited you." (Luke 19:44, NLT)

Was there another opportunity for those who decided not to go with the wise men?
What did the wise men gain from their adventure?
How did this adventure set them apart from others?

DISCUSSION QUESTIONS AND ACTIVITIES

Where have all the wise men gone?

- In small groups and develop a list of five public figures that you believe are wise.
- Select the public figure that you believe is the wisest person on your list.
- Identify the most admirable quality of the person selected.
- Identify what it takes to be wise? Courage, time, study, emulation of others?
- Reconvene. Have one group serve as "judge and jury" to evaluate presentations.
- The group judging will listen to the presentations, pose any questions, and render an opinion.
- The whole class will then vote for the wisest person discussed.

Objective: To identify and clarify wise attributes and why they are admirable.

What are you going to do about it?

The thing that set the wise men apart from other knowledgeable men and women is that they **acted** on their knowledge.

There were scholars right there in Israel who knew that the prophets foretold Bethlehem as the birthplace of the Messiah. Yet, despite the magnificent star, they did not worship. The wise men, however, made a long and demanding trip to visit the Lord.

- Is knowledge valuable if you don't apply it?
- Bethlehem is only five miles from Jerusalem! What does that say about the scribes?

Objective: To stir to action.

THE BIBLE ON WISDOM

I. The BIBLICAL DEFINITION of WISDOM: Behold, the fear of the Lord, that is wisdom; and **to depart** from evil is understanding. (Job 28:28). In other words, wisdom is **action**. The popular notion that wisdom concerns only the intellect is wrong. "The wisdom that comes from above is first of all pure and full of quiet gentleness. Then it is peace-loving and courteous. It allows discussion and is willing to yield to others; it is full of mercy and good deeds. It is wholehearted and straightforward and sincere." (James 3:17, 18, TLB)

II. BENEFITS OF WISDOM

(1) **PROTECTION.** For wisdom and truth will enter the very center of your being, filling your life with joy. You will be given the sense to stay away from evil men. (Proverbs 2:10-12, TLB)

(2) **HAPPINESS.** Happy is the man that finds wisdom, and the man that gets understanding. (Proverbs. 3:13)

(3) **LIFE, GRACE, and SAFETY.** Keep sound wisdom and discretion: So shall they be life unto your soul, and grace to your neck. Then shall you walk in your way safely, and your foot shall not stumble. (Proverbs 3:21-22)

(4) **PROMOTION and HONOR.** Exalt her, and she shall promote you: she shall bring you to honor, when you embrace her. (Proverbs 4:8)

(5) JUDGMENT. By me kings reign, and princes decree justice. By me princes rule, and nobles, even all the judges of the earth. (Proverbs 8:15-16)

(6) RECOGNITION. A man shall be commended according to his wisdom. (Proverbs 12:8)

(7) INSIGHT. Wisdom is of more value than foolishness, just as light is better than darkness; for the wise man sees, while the fool is blind. (Ecclesiastes 2:13)

III. WISDOM.

(1) Starting Point: The foundation of understanding Wisdom is knowing that God is in charge. He "made heaven and earth, the sea, and all that *is* in them." (Psalm 146:6, NKJV)

    a. How can men be wise? <u>The only way to begin is by reverence for God.</u> For growth in wisdom comes from obeying his laws. (Psalm 111:10, TLB)

    b. The fear of the Lord is the instruction of wisdom; and before honor is humility. (Proverbs 15:33)

(2) Where can we find wisdom?

    a. For **the Lord** gives wisdom. (Proverbs 2:6)

    b. When pride comes, then comes shame: but **with the lowly is wisdom**. (Proverbs 11:2)

    c. Only by pride comes contention: but **with the well advised is wisdom**. (Proverbs 13:10)

d. Now if any of you lacks wisdom, let him ask from God, the *One* giving generously to all and not finding fault, and it will be given to him.. (James 1:5, BLB)

(3) Wisdom is the main thing.

    a. Wisdom is the **principal** thing; therefore get wisdom: and with all your getting get understanding. (Proverbs 4:7)

    b. **How much better is it to get wisdom than gold!** (Proverbs 16:16)

    c. Wisdom is the main pursuit of sensible men. (Proverbs 17:24, TLB)

(4) Wisdom invites you to be wise.

    a. Does not wisdom cry? And understanding put forth her voice? She stands in the top of high places, by the way in the places of the paths. She cries at the gates, at the entry of the city, at the coming in at the doors. Unto you, O men, I call; and my voice is to the sons of man. (Proverbs 8:1-4)

    b. I love all who love me. Those who search for me shall surely find me. (Proverbs 8:17)

(5) The wise are profitable, but the foolish are punished and die.

    a. In the lips of him that has understanding wisdom is found: but **a rod is for the back of him that is void of understanding.** (Proverbs 10:13)

b. The lips of the righteous feed many: but **fools die for want of wisdom**. (Proverbs 10:21)

Matthew 7:24-27: Therefore whosoever hears these sayings of mine, and <u>does them</u>, I will liken him unto **a wise man**, which built his house upon a rock: And the rain descended, and the floods came, and the winds blew, and beat upon that house; and it fell not: for it was founded upon a rock. And every one that hears these sayings of mine, and does them not, shall be likened unto a **foolish man**, which built his house upon the sand: And the rain descended, and the floods came, and the winds blew, and beat upon that house; and it fell: and great was the fall of it.

IV.   APPLICATION: How long do you have to live wisely?

a. **We should make King David's prayer our own**: So teach us to number our days, **that we may apply** our hearts unto wisdom. (Psalms 90:12)
b. **We should also adopt David's attitude toward God**: As the hart pants after the water brooks, so pants my soul after you, Oh God. (Ps 42:1)
c. **Our wisdom should show up in how we live**: If you are wise, live a life of steady goodness, so that only good deeds will pour forth. And if you don't brag about them, then you will be truly wise! (James 3:13b, TLB)

THE ALTERNATIVE TO WISDOM IS FOOLISHNESS.

The consequences of lacking wisdom are severe. Foolishness is ignorance. "A foolish woman is clamorous: she is simple, and knows nothing." (Psalm 9:13). Another consequence is alienation from God. "The foolish shall not stand in your sight." (Psalms 5:5).

**And I saw that there is an advantage to wisdom above folly, like the advantage of the light above the darkness.
(Ecclesiastes 2:13, YLT)**

HOW TO BE WISE

- **MAKE WISDOM YOUR HIGHEST TOP PRIORITY.**

Getting wisdom is the most important thing you can do! (Proverbs 4:7, TLB).

There is really only one thing worth being concerned about. (Luke 10:42, TLB)

Love wisdom like a sweetheart. (Proverbs 7:4, TLB)

For such wisdom is far more valuable than precious jewels.

Nothing else compares with it. (Proverbs 3:15, TLB)

Recognize that wisdom is more than knowledge. It is knowledge put into action.

- **ASK GOD FOR WISDOM.**

For the LORD gives wisdom; From His mouth *come* knowledge and understanding.
(Proverbs 2:6, NKJV)

If you want to know what God wants you to do, **ask him**, and he will gladly tell you, for he is always ready to give a bountiful supply of wisdom to all who ask him; he will not resent it. (James 1:5, TLB).

You do not have because you do not ask. (James 4.2, NKJV).

- **MEDITATE ON THE WORD OF GOD.**

Study it **day and night.** Then you can be sure to obey what is written there. If you do this, you will be wise and successful in everything you do. (Joshua 1:8, ERV)

They love the LORD's teachings and think about them **day and night**. (Ps 1:2, ERV)

I will instruct you and teach you in the way you should go; I will counsel you with my eye upon you. (Psalm 32:8, ESV).

Your word is a lamp for my feet and a light on my path. (Psalm 119:105, CSB)

Every word of God proves true. (Proverbs 30:5, NLT)

Your words came to me, and I ate them up. (Jeremiah 15:16, ERV)

Man shall not live by bread alone, but by every word of God. (Luke 4:4, KJV)

All Scripture is breathed out by God and profitable for teaching, for reproof, for correction, and for training in righteousness. (2 Timothy 3:16).

- **SPEND TIME WITH GODLY PEOPLE. ONLY GODLY PEOPLE CAN GIVE GOOD ADVICE.**

A godly man gives good advice. (Prov. 10:21, TLB)

He who walks with wise *men* will be wise. (Proverbs 13:20, NKJV)

- **AVOID UNGODLY PEOPLE.**

Good people have kind thoughts, but you should never trust the advice of someone evil. (Proverbs 12:5, CEV)

The thoughts of the righteous are just; the counsels of the wicked are deceitful. (Proverbs 12:28, ESV).

Don't let others spoil your faith and joy with their philosophies, their wrong and shallow answers built on men's thoughts and ideas, instead of on what Christ has said. (Colossians 2:8, TLB).

- **FEAR AND OBEY GOD.**

The fear of the Lord is the beginning of knowledge. (Proverbs 1:7, ESV)

If you love me, you will do what I have said, and my Father will love you. I will also love you and show you what I am like. (John 14:21, CEV)

And remember, it is a message to obey, not just to listen to. So don't fool yourselves. For if a person just listens and doesn't obey, he is like a man looking at his face in a mirror; as soon as he walks away, he can't see himself anymore or remember what he looks like. But if anyone keeps **looking steadily into God's law** for free men, he will not only remember it but he will do what it says, and God will **greatly bless** him in everything he does. (James 1:22-25, TLB).

- **PAY ATTENTINON TO WHAT YOU SEE and HEAR. AVOID DANGER.**

The wise man learns by listening; the simpleton can learn only by seeing scorners punished. (Proverbs 21:11, TLB)

- **REMEMBER THE BENEFITS OF WISDOM**

Have two goals: wisdom—that is, knowing and doing right—and common sense. Don't let them slip away, for they fill you with living energy and bring you honor and respect. (Proverbs 3:21-22, TLB).

The man who knows right from wrong and has good judgment and common sense is happier than the man who is immensely rich! For such wisdom is far more valuable than precious jewels. Nothing else compares with it. Wisdom gives: a long, good life, riches, honor, pleasure, peace. Wisdom is a tree of life to those who eat her fruit; happy is the man who keeps on eating it. (Proverbs 3:13-18, TLB)

The wise are promoted to honor. (Proverbs 3:35, TLB)

Do not forsake her—then she will guard you; love her and she will keep you.

(Proverbs 4:6, TLB)

If you exalt wisdom, she will exalt you. Hold her fast, and she will lead you to **great honor**; she will place a beautiful crown upon your head. (Proverbs 4:8-9, TLB)

Wisdom is more precious than rubies, and nothing you desire can compare with her. (Proverbs 8:11, NIV)

Wisdom is its own reward. (Proverbs 9:12, TLB)

Smart people are rewarded with knowledge. (Proverbs 14:18, ERV)

A wise person's reward is **wealth**. (Proverbs 14:24, ERV)

Your words are what sustain me; they are food to my hungry soul. They bring joy to my sorrowing heart and delight me. (Jeremiah 15:16, TLB)

I saw that wisdom is better than foolishness in the same way that light is better than darkness. (Ecclesiastes 2:13, ERV).

- **REMEMBER THE COSTS OF FOOLISHNESS**

My wounds stink and fester because of my foolishness. (Psalm 38:5 ESV)

Homes are made by the wisdom of women, but are destroyed by foolishness. (Proverbs 14:1).

- **IF YOU <u>APPLY</u> THE WISDOM YOU HAVE, GOD WILL GIVE YOU MORE.**

Tackle every task that comes along, and if you fear God, you can expect his blessing. (Ecclesiastes 7:18, TLB)

For whoever has, to him *more* will be given. (Luke 8:18, NKJV)

- **PAY TUITION. USE TIME WELL. LEARN IT ONCE. APPLY IT OVER AND OVER.**

Look carefully then how you walk, not as unwise but as wise, making the **best use of the time**, because the days are evil. (Ephesians 5:15-16, ESV)

- **DON'T BE EMBARRASSED TO ASK A QUESTION.**

The good man **asks advice** from friends; the wicked plunge ahead—and fall. (Proverbs 12:26)

The ear that listens to life-giving reproof will dwell among the wise. Whoever ignores instruction despises himself, but he who listens to reproof gains intelligence. The fear of the LORD is instruction in wisdom, and **humility** comes before honor. (Proverbs 15:31-33, ESV).

- **DON'T TALK SO MUCH.**

He who has knowledge spares his words, *and* a man of understanding is of a calm spirit. (Proverbs 17:27, NKJV)

Dear brothers, don't ever forget that it is best to listen much, speak little. (James 1:19).

- **STAY ON TRACK**

If you stop learning, you will forget what you already know. (Proverbs 19:27, CEV).

CHAPTER 10

THE EARLY CHURCH

A Study in Supernatural Power

But when the Holy Spirit has come upon you, you will receive power to testify about me with great effect, to the people in Jerusalem, throughout Judea, in Samaria, and to the ends of the earth, about my death and resurrection
Acts 1:8 TLB

The explosive growth of the early church is one of the most compelling stories ever recorded. Beginning with a small group of common men, the gospel quickly advanced throughout the middle east and Europe, touching beggars and barons, commoner and kings. Although the first soldiers of the cross were harassed, whipped, jailed, and executed, they continued to preach the gospel fearlessly. Most clearly, the Holy Spirit worked through these men, demonstrating the awesome power of God to a lost and dying world.

Jesus had foretold their plight in Luke 21: 12-16: "They will lay their hands on you and persecute you, delivering you up to the synagogues and prisons. You will be brought before kings and rulers for My name's sake. But it will turn out for you as an occasion for testimony. Therefore settle *it* in your hearts not to meditate beforehand on what you will ▫answer; for I will give you a mouth and wisdom which all your adversaries will not be able to contradict or ▫resist."

These men knew that scorn, hardship, and violence lay ahead, yet chose to obey the Lord's command to preach the truth of salvation to all men. They faced self-serving politicians, envious religious elders, angry mobs, and a warped legal system. Yet they succeeded in launching an international evangelistic campaign. These were ordinary men whom God used mightily, instruments of divine purpose, earthen vessels carrying the treasure of Christ.

Responsibility for the Church

Regarding the church, Jesus is the head, builder, Chief Cornerstone and foundation.

The church belongs to Jesus and he is responsible for her success. Before his crucifixion, Jesus stated, "<u>I will build my church</u>; and the gates of hell shall not prevail against it" (Matthew 16:18, KJV). Note that the church is on the offensive and the gates of hell are in a defensive posture.

Knowing that responsibility for building the church rests with Jesus, it is easy to see why miracles and signs accompanied the preaching of the gospel.

These signs and wonders served to confirm the gospel. When Jesus told the disciples to preach to the world, he reassured them of his presence and his power. "And Jesus came and spoke unto them, saying, All power is given unto me in heaven and in earth. … and, lo, I am with you always, even unto the end of the world. Amen" (Matthew 28: 18, 20, KJV).

In reviewing these great accomplishments, we are really reading about the Lord's work *through* his people. Jesus foretold great works. "Verily, verily, I say unto you, He that believes on me, the works that I do shall he do also; and *greater works than these shall he do*; because I go unto my Father" (John 14:12, KJV).

Jesus sent the Holy Spirit to empower the saints to do the work of God. "Nevertheless, I tell you the truth; It is expedient for you that I go away: for if I go not away, the Comforter will not come unto you; but if I depart, *I will send him unto you*. And when he is come, he will reprove the world of sin, and of righteousness, and of judgment: Of sin, because they believe not on me; of righteousness, because I go to my Father, and you see me no more; of judgment, because the prince of this world is judged" (John 16: 7-11, KJV).

Jesus is also the Chief Cornerstone (Matthew 21:42). As the Chief Cornerstone, all references, plans, and building are based on Christ's position. Growth will always be aligned with the Son of God's precepts and purpose.

Jesus is also the foundation of the church and supports the entire church. Paul talked about this when he described himself simply as a co-laborer with God. Paul made it clear that he was not the basis of the church. The apostle said that Christians truly belonged to God and that nothing could be built on any foundation other than Christ. "You are <u>God's</u> garden, not ours; you are <u>God's</u> building, not ours. … And no one can ever lay any other real foundation than that one we already have–Jesus Christ" (1 Corinthians 3: 9, 11, TLB).

Defining Attributes of the Early Church

The following eight attributes distinguished the body of Christ in the first century.

1. **Supernatural power**
2. **Divine guidance**
3. **Opportunistic preaching**
4. **Boldness**
5. **Specialized teams**
6. **Love for other Christians**
7. **Endurance**
8. **Focus on the eternal**

Again and again, the first evangelists exemplified these attributes as they battled jealous religious leaders, demented rulers, greedy businessmen, and demonic forces. Yet, God's supernatural power and continual guidance resulted in bold, undeterred, and committed men and women who carried the gospel to a world starved for truth. These giants of our faith were able to endure enormous hardship because of their love for others and their focus on heaven.

The Beginning and the Infilling (Acts 1 and 2)

After Jesus was resurrected, he visited his disciples, breathing on them and saying, "Receive the Holy Ghost" (John 20:22, KJV). But even though they received the Holy Ghost when Jesus breathed on them, Jesus told them to wait for the filling of the Holy Ghost in Jerusalem. This second experience of the Baptism of the Holy Spirit would fill them with "power from on high" (Luke 24:49, KJV).

The first Christians never could have evangelized such a large region of the world using only the skills acquired from their work in fishing, tax collecting, and the like. For this undertaking, they needed the supernatural power which Jesus had promised. The Lord's promise was fulfilled with the outpouring of the Holy Spirit in Jerusalem on the day of Pentecost. "And when the day of Pentecost was fully come, they were all with one accord in one place. And suddenly there came a sound from heaven as of a rushing mighty wind, and it filled all the house where they were sitting. And there appeared unto them cloven tongues like as of fire, and it sat upon each of them. And they were all filled with the Holy Ghost, and began to speak with other tongues, as the Spirit gave them utterance" (Acts 2: 1-4, KJV).

The church had received supernatural power to embark upon the great commission to reach the entire world. Pentecost marked the birth of the Church.

Powerful Preaching and Healings (Acts 2 and 4)

To explain this mighty outpouring of the Holy Spirit, Peter preached his first sermon. He told the men of Judea that the tongues they heard had been prophesied by Joel: "… this is that which was spoken by the prophet Joel; And it shall come to pass in the last days, said God, I will pour out of my Spirit upon all flesh" (Acts 2:16-17, KJV). Peter's piercing sermon resulted in 3,000 people accepting Christ. What a glorious beginning for the new church!

Fellowship, Miracles, and Converts (Acts 2)

These new Christians also wanted to be with other believers as they grew in the new faith. "And they continued steadfastly in the apostles' doctrine and fellowship, and in breaking of bread, and in prayers. And fear came upon every soul: and many *wonders and signs were done by the apostles*" (Acts 2:42-43, KJV). These signs and wonders attracted attention to the message of salvation.

Shortly thereafter, Peter and John found a man at the temple who had been crippled his entire life. Peter said, "Silver and gold have I none; but such as I have give I you: In the name of Jesus Christ of Nazareth rise up and walk. And he took him by the right hand, and lifted him up: and immediately his feet and ankle bones received strength. And he leaping up stood, and walked, and entered with them into the temple, walking, and leaping, and praising God. And all the people saw him walking and praising God" (Acts 3: 6-9, KJV).

Naturally, when a crowd gathered to see the healed man, Peter seized the opportunity to preach. Many people accepted his message and the church grew to about 5,000 members. Thus, Peter's first two sermons attracted about 8,000 new Christians. The Church was off to a fast start!

Face Off with Religious Leaders (Acts 4)

However, the Jewish leaders were very upset about Peter proclaiming that Jesus had risen from the dead and they hauled Peter and John in to jail. They soon summoned them for questioning about the healing of the lame man: "By what power, or by what name, have you done this?" (Acts 4:7). But Peter viewed this as another opportunity to preach and he, *filled with the Holy Spirit*, testified to them about Christ, giving credit to God for the healing of the lame man and pointing to Christ as the only way to salvation.

"Now when they saw the **boldness** of Peter and John, and perceived that they were unlearned and ignorant men, they marveled; and they took knowledge of them, that they had been with Jesus" (Acts 4:13, KJV). Peter and John made an impression, not by the way they dressed, nor by their education or wealth. They impressed the court with their **boldness**.

Peter and John knew the power of God firsthand and the Holy Spirit was working *through* them, testifying of Christ.

The Pharisees and elders represented the highest echelon of Jewish society. Resistance at this level compelled the apostles to pray urgently for more power to accomplish the task of evangelism. They prayed for healings, signs and wonders and to preach with "**all boldness**" (Acts 4:29). Following their prayer, the building shook, and they proclaimed the word of God with power. The disciples "were of one heart and one soul. … And with great power gave the apostles witness of the resurrection of the Lord Jesus: and great grace was upon them all" (Acts 4: 32-33, KJV). God generously provided the apostles with more than enough power for the task. Right away, this two-man team of Peter and John had a dramatic impact as a result of supernatural power, divine guidance, and **boldness**. God always equips his people to carry out their tasks.

Honesty Required (Acts 5: 1-11)

The Holy Spirit worked supernaturally in the early church to crush deceit. A husband and his wife sold a plot of land and the man informed Peter that the entire amount from the sale was being given. However, God revealed the falsehood to Peter who **boldly** confronted him, "You have not lied unto men, but unto God" (Acts 5:4, KJV). Because of his dishonesty, he died and was carried off by some of the men in church. Immediately thereafter, his wife appeared to carry on their plot, but she also fell dead at Peter's feet and was carried away by the same men. This proved to the church, and everyone around, that God knew the motives of men. It also proved that the church was not governed by mere men, but by God Himself. From this episode, we see that God's divine guidance and supernatural power were exercised in the judgment of transgressors within the church. Once again, news of this event spread rapidly among the church and the community, attracting a great deal of attention.

Signs and Wonders (Acts 5: 12-16)

The Holy Spirit performed many signs and wonders through the apostles, from which they gained great admiration among the people and won many converts. The power of the Holy Spirit was upon Peter in such an awesome way that the sick were healed when his shadow passed over them! Multitudes came from surrounding cities to be healed and delivered from demons, and "they were healed every one" (Acts 5:16).

More Friction, More Boldness (Acts 5: 17-42)

With everyone thronging to the apostles, the Jewish religious leaders became extremely jealous and decided to throw them in jail. "But the angel of the Lord by night opened the prison doors, and brought them forth, and said, Go, stand and speak in the temple to the people all the words of this life" (Acts 5:19-20, KJV).

So, the apostles went to the temple in Jerusalem early the next morning and began to preach. Subsequently, when the authorities brought them in for questioning, Peter responded with a sermon to these men, who were "cut to the heart, and took counsel to slay them" (Acts 5:33, KJV).

However, at the last moment, wisdom prevailed. Gamaliel, a respected lawyer and teacher, stood up and warned the council to be careful how they treated the apostles. "But if it is of God, you cannot overthrow it; lest haply you be found even to fight against God" (Acts 5:39, KJV). The religious leaders accepted his advice and, after beating the apostles, let them go.

The apostles left "rejoicing that they were counted worthy to suffer shame for his name" (Acts 5:41, KJV). They were committed to their mission, regardless of the disapproval of the local religious authorities. The apostles viewed poor treatment as an honor and suffering for which they would surely be rewarded in heaven. Paul would later describe his hardships as a "light affliction, which is but for a moment" (2 Cor 4:17).

"And daily in the temple, and in every house, they ceased not to teach and preach Jesus Christ" (Acts 5:42, KJV). Amidst all this adversity, they remained undeterred in proclaiming the truth of Jesus Christ.

Managing Growth (Acts 6)

After the number of Christians had grown tremendously, the apostles had to settle a domestic problem. Church members were sharing food, but a group of Greek widows were not receiving a fair share. So, the apostles appointed seven godly men to oversee the distribution of provisions. This allowed the apostles to devote themselves "continually to prayer, and to the ministry of the word" (Acts 6:4, KJV).

The apostles' teaching and preaching brought church growth: "And the word of God increased; and the number of the disciples multiplied in Jerusalem greatly; and a great company of the priests were obedient to the faith" (Acts 6:7, KJV).

The Cost of Godliness (Acts 7)

Stephen, a man full of faith and power, had the singular honor of being the first martyr of the church. When the ungodly failed to match his wisdom and reason, they resorted to violence. Yet even as they hurled stones at him, Stephen reflected the love of Christ with his last words, "Lord, lay not this sin to their charge" (Acts 7:60, KJV).

Demons Stumble. Crippled Walk to Victory. (Acts 8)

Once again, miracles provided the proof of the message of salvation to a new group of people. The Samaritans accepted the gospel because of the healings and wonders done by Philip. "Then Philip went down to the city of Samaria, and preached Christ unto them. And the people with one accord gave heed unto those things which Philip spoke, hearing and seeing the miracles which he did. For unclean spirits, crying with loud voice, came out of many that were possessed with them: and many taken with palsies, and that were lame, were healed. And there was great joy in that city" (Acts 8: 5-8, KJV).

Hearing this wonderful news, the other apostles sent Peter and John to teach these new converts and pray for them to be baptized in the Holy Spirit, "(For as yet he was fallen upon none of them: only they were baptized in the name of the Lord Jesus.) Then laid they their hands on them, and they received the Holy Ghost" (Acts 8:16-17, KJV).

A High Official Receives Christ (Acts 8: 26-39)

Later, Philip, at the direction of an angel, met the treasurer of Ethiopia. He had been reading the prophecies of Isaiah and asked Philip to explain them. Philip told him that Isaiah prophesied about the Messiah. When they found some water by the road, the treasurer asked why he could not be baptized right then and there.

"And Philip said, 'If you believe with all your heart, you may.'

And he answered and said, 'I believe that Jesus Christ is the Son of God.'

And he commanded the chariot to stand still: and they went down both into the water, both Philip and the eunuch; and he baptized him. And when they were come up out of the water, the Spirit of the Lord caught away Philip, that the eunuch saw him no more: and he went on his way rejoicing. But Philip was found at Azotus: and passing through he preached in all the cities, until he came to Caesarea" (Acts 8:37-40, KJV).

From Ferocious Adversary to Chief Advocate (Acts 8:1-4; 9: 1-22)

Saul, a highly educated and zealous Pharisee, began to arrest and jail believers. Under this great persecution, many Christians fled Jerusalem for distant lands. On the way, they spread the gospel to those they met. They also established churches in their new locations.

As Saul was on his way to Damascus to arrest Christians, the Lord blinded him and said, "I am Jesus whom you persecute. ... And he trembling and astonished said, Lord, what will you have me to do? And the Lord said unto him, Arise, and go into the city, and it shall be told you what you must do" (Acts 9: 5-6, KJV).

Saul responded to Jesus by calling him "Lord."

God instructed a Christian in Damascus, by the name of Ananias, to pray for Paul. The Lord also gave Saul a vision of this man laying his hand on him to restore his eyesight. God informed Ananias that Saul was "a chosen vessel unto me, to bear my name before the Gentiles, and kings, and the children of Israel: For I will show him how great things he must suffer for my name's sake. And Ananias went his way, and entered into the house; and putting his hands on him said, Brother Saul, the Lord, even Jesus, that appeared unto you in the way as you came, has sent me, that you might receive your sight, and be filled with the Holy Ghost. And immediately there fell from his eyes as it had been scales: and he received sight forthwith, and arose, and was baptized" (Acts 9: 15-18, KJV).

Saul, also known as Paul, immediately went to the synagogues of Damascus and began preaching that Jesus is the Son of God. Given his harsh persecution of the church in the past, people were skeptical. Nevertheless, Paul kept on preaching and proving to the Jews that Jesus is the Son of God. The confounded Jews plotted to kill him but Paul became aware of their plan. Paul made it to safety one night when his disciples lowered him over the city wall in a basket.

Later, in Jerusalem, Paul argued with the Greeks about the deity of Christ until he became aware of yet another plot against his life. The disciples sent him to Tarsus.

Three Towns Won to Christ (Acts 9: 34-43)

As he was traveling through a town, Peter came upon a man who had been bed-ridden with palsy for eight years. "Peter said to him, 'Aeneas, Jesus the Christ heals you. Arise and make your bed.' Then he arose immediately" (Acts 9:34, KJV). Two nearby towns saw this man after he was healed and everyone turned to the Lord.

After this, while Peter was in Lydda, two men came to ask him to come with them. Peter agreed and traveled to Joppa, where they showed him the body of a just-departed saint named Tabitha. Peter told everyone to leave the room, knelt down, and prayed. He then turned to Tabitha's dead body and commanded: "Tabitha, arise. And she opened her eyes: and when she saw Peter, she sat up" (Acts 9:40, KJV). This resurrection became known all over town and brought many to accept Christ as Lord.

Divine Orders for an Army Captain (Acts 10:1-48)

One afternoon in Caesarea, a devout and upright military captain named Cornelius saw an angel. The angel told him to ask Peter to come and teach him. So, Cornelius sent three men for Peter.

Although the angel could have instructed Cornelius himself, God wanted to use Peter so that Peter would realize that salvation was available to gentiles.

The day following Cornelius' vision, Peter also had a vision. He saw a sheet full of all sorts of animals coming down from heaven. Then a voice told Peter to rise, kill and eat. But he objected because he had never eaten anything except food approved by Jewish law. But the voice spoke a second time, saying, "What God has cleansed, that call not common" (Acts 10:15, KJV). This was done three times and the sheet, containing all different kinds of animals, was taken back up to heaven.

Peter was mulling over the dream's meaning when Cornelius' men appeared at the front gate. The next day, Peter and a few other Christians went to Cornelius' home.

Upon entering the home, Peter found a large group of people waiting for him. He reminded them that it was against Jewish law for him to associate with Gentiles, but that God had revealed to him that all men were now clean. When Peter asked Cornelius why he had been invited, Cornelius recounted the vision of the angel.

Peter began to expound upon the Lord and the Holy Ghost fell upon the group and they began to speak in tongues and praise God. Peter said, "Can any man forbid water, that these should not be baptized, which have received the Holy Ghost as well as we? And he commanded them to be baptized in the name of the Lord" (Acts 10:47-48, KJV).

To arrange the remarkable meeting between Peter, a Jew, and Cornelius, a Gentile, God employed supernatural means. He used an angel to instruct Cornelius so that when Peter heard Cornelius' story, he would know that this was of God. God used a vision to instruct Peter, because no human being could have convinced Peter to interact with Gentiles. Even then, Peter needed to see the vision three times! His zealous personality and strict training would have prevented such association with gentiles. Perhaps God used Cornelius and Peter to bring the gospel to the Gentiles because both were credible and respected men.

Another Breakthrough: More Gentiles Converted! (Acts 11: 19-30)

As a result of the severe persecution in Jerusalem that had cost Stephen his life, many Christians fled to other cities. When these Jewish Christians reached Antioch, they preached to the Greeks also; and a great many accepted Christ as Lord and Savior. When the Christians in Jerusalem heard this news, they sent Barnabas to Antioch where he exhorted the disciples to stay close to God and won many more to Christ.

Barnabas then went to Tarsus and returned to Antioch with Saul. They remained there for one year, teaching and preaching. Antioch was the first place that believers were called Christians.

The Cruelty of King Herod (Acts 12:1-24)

The Roman ruler Herod decided to attack the church and executed John's brother James by sword. Because this pleased the Jews, Herod arrested Peter also. But an angel appeared in Peter's cell and awakened him with a slap on the side. The chains fell off and the angel commanded Peter to hurry and get dressed and to follow him. Peter followed him out of the prison to the gate, which opened supernaturally. Peter was free! The angel walked with him for a block and then departed. Peter soon went to the home of Mary, John Mark's mother, where Christians were gathered together praying for him. He explained what had happened and they were utterly shocked and joyful. "But the word of God grew and multiplied" (Acts 12:24, KJV). Neither martyrdom, nor imprisonment, nor the loss of great men of God could stop the advance of the gospel.

Guidance from The Holy Ghost (Acts 13: 1-14)

The church often prayed and fasted for the guidance of the Holy Spirit.

Acts 13 records specific instructions from the Holy Spirit to the Antioch church. "As they ministered to the Lord, and fasted, the Holy Ghost said, 'Separate me Barnabas and Saul for the work whereunto I have called them.' And when they had fasted and prayed, and laid their hands on them, they sent them away. So they, being sent forth by the Holy Ghost, departed" (Acts 13:1-4, KJV).

Perhaps the Holy Spirit designated Paul and Barnabas because they had the background and training to travel to distant lands and understand new cultures. Paul was highly educated and multilingual. The church at Antioch received a message from the Holy Spirit to "Separate me Barnabas and Saul for the work whereunto I have called them" (Acts 13:2, KJV). *The Holy Spirit did not mention John Mark.* Later in the journey, when Paul and Barnabas sailed to Turkey, John Mark abandoned the mission and went back home to Jerusalem. Thus, the guidance of the Holy Spirit proved true.

Paul's First Missionary Journey (Acts 13)

Nevertheless, Paul, Barnabas and John Mark left their home church and began a journey that would take them through many perilous places. Paul began preaching in the Syrian port city of Seleucia. He then sailed to the island of Cypress, where he preached from town to town.

A Sorcerer Blinded. A Governor's Eyes Opened (Acts 13: 5-12)

Next, under the guidance of the Holy Spirit, he traveled to a town called Paphos.

There Paul and his companions encountered a false prophet. This sorcerer argued with them as they were trying to persuade the governor to accept Christ. Paul turned upon the sorcerer and pronounced the judgment of God upon him: "You child of the devil, you enemy of all righteousness, will you not cease to pervert the right ways of the Lord? And now, behold, the hand of the Lord is upon you, and you shall be blind, not seeing the sun for a season. And immediately there fell on him a mist and a darkness; and he went about seeking some to lead him by the hand" (Acts 13: 9-11, KJV). It was clear to the deputy that Paul's God was more powerful than that of the sorcerer. "Then the deputy, when he saw what was done, believed, being astonished at the doctrine of the Lord" (Acts 13:12).

Hungry People. Fed Up Leaders (Acts 13: 14-44)

From Paphos, Paul, Barnabas and John Mark sailed to Turkey. In Paul's first sermon in Turkey, he spoke at length in the synagogue and was asked to return the following Sabbath. On this occasion, almost everyone in the city came to hear Paul. But because of the great following, the Jewish leaders became jealous and began to berate and curse Paul. As a result, Paul turned away from the Jews and focused on the Gentiles, many of whom believed. But the Jews stirred up a mob which hounded Paul and Barnabas out of town, who upon their departure, shook off the dust of their feet as a testimony against them.

Iconium Divided into Two Camps (Acts 14:1-7)

Next, in Iconium, Paul and Barnabas both preached powerfully in the local synagogue, converting large numbers of Jews and Greeks. However, part of the Jewish citizenry remained entrenched against them and started rumors about them among the Gentiles. Yet God justified their message with many miracles among the people and they stayed there a "long time...speaking boldly in the Lord" (Acts 14:3, KJV).

Iconium's priests and elders viewed the preaching of this new doctrine of salvation as an offense worthy of death. They devised a plan to form an angry mob that would stone Paul and Barnabas. To avoid death, they fled to Lystra.

Loved in Lystra (Acts 14:8-17)

In Lystra, Paul saw a crippled man and, noticing his faith, commanded him to get up. The man not only stood up, but leaped and began to walk. This miracle of healing astonished the city because the man had been crippled from birth. The awestruck citizens concluded that Paul and Barnabas were gods in human form. Even the local pagan priest brought them cart loads of flowers and wanted to sacrifice oxen to them! Paul and Barnabas were quite upset about the uproar and tried to turn them to God. Even so, the citizens treated them as near divine.

Hated in Lystra (Acts 14: 19-20)

Within a few days, however, the adulation turned to contempt when malevolent Jews who had been tracking Paul showed up. They incited a mob that stoned Paul and, believing him to be dead, dragged him out of the city. Yet, once Paul regained consciousness, he got up and went right back into Lystra and spent the night!

Public opinion, whether adverse or supportive, did not deter Paul from his work. He remained bold and committed to his ministry despite accusation and injury.

Winning Derbe. Strengthening Others.
(Acts 14:20-26)

The following day, Paul and Barnabas traveled to Derbe where they won many people to Christ. After preaching and teaching the next day, they returned to Lystra, Iconium, and Antioch of Prisidia, home of the same malicious elements that had just attacked them! Having just survived a stoning, Paul's credibility and testimony were extremely strong. To encourage these new Christians, Paul and Barnabas told them that "we must through much tribulation enter into the kingdom of God" (Acts 14:22). In addition to the encouragement and exhortation provided, they also appointed elders in the churches. Not only did Paul and Barnabas plant the churches, they also ordained shepherds to care for the congregations.

Paul and Barnabas could have simply preached salvation in these cities, leaving them to fend for themselves, but it is clear that they valued these men and women as spiritual offspring. Church planting was only the first step in their missionary work. Follow-up, exhortation, and teaching were also an integral part of their ministry. They were wise to show the churches the specific steps in living the Christian life. Before leaving, they prayed for the Christians and committed them to the care of the Lord.

Paul and Barnabas continued their journey through several cities and preached in Perga before sailing back home to Antioch at last. When they arrived, they called the congregation together to recant the glorious work of the Lord on their journey and tell of the Gentiles' acceptance of the gospel. These well-traveled missionaries remained at their home church in Antioch for a lengthy stay.

A Word about Barnabas (Acts 4, 9, 11)

While Paul is much more widely known because of his writings, it should be noted that Barnabas was a significant figure in this evangelical campaign. Baranabas, like many lesser known Christians during this period, played crucial roles in the establishment of the church. The fact that he was somewhat less visible than Paul does not diminish his tremendous contribution to God's work.

Barnabas was a generous and compassionate man who had sold his land and donated the money to the church. The apostles gave him a surname meaning "the son of consolation" (Acts 4:36, KJV).

Barnabas was a critical partner with Paul and served several key roles in Paul's success. First of all, it was Barnabas who vouched for Paul's conversion to the apostles. Given Paul's violent history of persecuting Christians, he needed someone with an exemplary reputation to confirm that his conversion was genuine. "But Barnabas took him, and brought him to the apostles, and declared unto them how he had seen the Lord in the way, and that he had spoken to him, and how he had preached boldly at Damascus in the name of Jesus" (Acts 9:27, KJV).

Secondly, it was Barnabas who first brought Paul to Antioch, the home church from which Paul ministered: "Then departed Barnabas to Tarsus, for to seek Saul: And when he had found him, he brought him unto Antioch. And it came to pass, that a whole year they assembled themselves with the church, and taught much people" (Acts 11: 25-26, KJV).

And, of course, Barnabas accompanied Paul on his first missionary journey, preaching powerfully, praying continually; a constant companion to Paul in both joy and pain. Furthermore, when Paul conducted his second journey .Barnabas embarked upon a missionary journey himself.

The secret of the successful evangelist is found in Barnabas. He had three personal attributes to attract the lost: goodness, power, and faith. "For he was a good man, full of the Holy Spirit and of faith. And a great many people were added to the Lord." (Acts 11:24, NKJV).

Other Missionary Teams (Acts 15)

Paul and Barnabas were not the only ministers in peril. Judas and Silas were "men who have risked their lives for the name of our Lord Jesus Christ." (Acts 15:26). Despite widespread and vicious persecution, many others were committed to preaching the gospel. Some are mentioned only briefly in scripture and many are not recorded at all. God's plan included a growing body of believers who would all testify to the good news of salvation. He never intended for only one or two "stars" to evangelize the world by themselves. Everyone has a role to play.

The Holy Spirit Forms Church Doctrine (Acts 15)

In forming church doctrine, the council acknowledged the guidance of the Holy Spirit in their decision and action: "For it seemed good to the Holy Ghost, and to us, to lay upon you no greater burden than these necessary things" (Acts 15:28, KJV). The church was learning as it grew. Sound doctrine was published, namely that non-Jewish Christians were under no obligation to keep Jewish laws.

The church founders realized that divine, commonly held doctrine was essential for unity and that all churches needed to know the principles of the faith agreed upon by the elders and apostles. Internal organization and understanding sustained the evangelical outreach of the early church.

Still on Paul's Heart (Acts 15:36)

Not long after the declaration of church doctrine regarding gentile Christians (that they not be required to comply with Jewish laws), Paul suggested to Barnabas that they return to the churches they had planted to see how they were doing. This meant another long, hard journey, but Paul had a strong desire to see them face to face. However, while making travel plans, Paul and Barnabas, two men with great respect for one another, had a strong disagreement about who should go with them. Paul refused to let John Mark come along because he had turned back on their first trip. In the end Paul split from Barnabas and took a devout man named Silas with him.

Paul's Second Missionary Journey (Acts 16:1-4)

Paul and Silas first visited Derbe and then Lystra, where they met Timothy, a highly respected man who agreed to join them in their work. They traveled to the various churches to explain the doctrine set by the apostles and elders in Jerusalem.

The addition of Timothy to Paul's small ministerial team was a significant event. Paul would later say in his letter to the Philippians that he had no one else like Timothy, who had a natural care for others.

The Holy Spirit Determines Where to Minister (Acts 16)

Paul, Silas and Timothy were "forbidden of the Holy Ghost to preach the word in Asia" (Acts 16:6). They then headed toward Bythynia, but the Holy Spirit denied this destination as well.

But Paul soon had a vision of a man in Macedonia asking for Paul to come and help them. They obeyed immediately, "So we[a] decided to leave for Macedonia at once, having concluded that God was calling us to preach the Good News there" (Acts 16:10, TLB). God guided them continually and clearly.

Supernatural Works (Acts 16:11-33)

They went to Philippi, the most important city in the region, and attended a Sabbath prayer meeting on the outskirts of the town. There they spoke to a salesperson named Lydia and the Lord opened her heart to accept Christ. Both she and her whole household were baptized!

Later, in Philippi, they encountered a young girl who was possessed by an evil spirit. The devil prompted the girl to tell the future and had made a great deal of money for her managers. Paul, in the name of Jesus Christ, commanded the spirit of divination to come out of her. Her managers flew into a rage because of the loss of profit and persuaded the local authorities to confine and whip Paul and Silas.

While in jail, Paul and Silas sang praises to God and about midnight, God sent an earthquake. It shook the foundations of the prison, flinging every door open. The jail keeper saw all this, and thinking the prisoners had escaped, prepared to kill himself. But Paul shouted to him not to harm himself and assured him that no one had fled. He then testified to the jailer, resulting in his conversion and that of each family member!

The following day, when the authorities sent word to let Paul and Silas go, Paul informed them that he and Silas were both Roman citizens and had been whipped without a fair trial. He then demanded that the authorities free them in person. Upon hearing this, they rushed over and released Paul and Silas, begging them to leave town. After encouraging the Christians in Philippi, Paul and Silas departed.

Eventually, Paul continued his travels to Corinth accompanied by Aquila and Priscilla, a Christian couple who were tent makers like Paul. They were a great help to Paul in ministry, fellowship, and vocation. Subsequently, Paul traveled to Ephesus and debated with those who attended the synagogue. Although they wanted him to stay longer, Paul sailed to Caesarea, where he visited the church before returning to Antioch.

Preaching and Uproar. Preaching and Uproar. (Acts 17:1 – 19:41)

As usual opposition their preaching met opposition in Thessalonica, Berea, Athens, Corinth, and Ephesus.

When Paul reached Thessalonica, he went to the synagogue to debate about Christ. A large number of people who heard Paul believed his message and accepted the Lord; but, as usual, the Jewish leaders became jealous. They stirred up a mob that dragged some Christians before the city's rulers, shouting: "These that have turned the world upside down are come hither also" (Acts 17:6, KJV). These early missionaries were known throughout the region.

After the Christians paid the authorities, Paul and Silas left for Berea. In Berea, Paul preached in the synagogue and many Jews believed him. These Jews at Berea were more noble than the other churches because they verified Paul's sermons by researching the scriptures to verify what they had heard. But unbelieving Jews from Thessalonica caught up with Paul and caused trouble. Paul left by sea.

In Athens, Paul was aroused by the rampant idol worship all around him. In his usual manner, Paul debated with the idolaters in the synagogue and in the marketplace. At the request of the local philosophers, Paul decided to give a speech to the Athenians. Having noticed that they had constructed a statue to the "Unknown God," Paul picked up on this idea and gave a skillful oration, proclaiming that their Unknown God was in fact Jesus Christ. After debunking the notion of gods made of silver and gold, Paul began to talk about the resurrection of the dead, which most of the philosophers rejected. Even among this misguided group, Paul found a handful of people who accepted Christ.

In Corinth, they again preached in the synagogue, and again, the Jews resisted them. But there was a devout man living next to the synagogue who lodged Paul. So Paul continued preaching. Soon, the ruler of the synagogue accepted Christ, opening the door for many Jews to come forward. "One night the Lord spoke to Paul in a vision and told him, 'Don't be afraid! Speak out! Don't be silent! For I am with you, and no one will attack and harm you, for many people in this city belong to me.' So Paul stayed there for the next year and a half, teaching the word of God." (Acts 18:9-11, TLB)

Later, the Jews would bring another accusation against Paul, but it was thrown out of court. Eventually, when Paul left Corinth, the husband and wife ministry team of Priscilla and Aquila accompanied him to the port city of Ephesus. Upon arrival in Ephesus, Paul urgently located the local synagogue and began to preach.

Good Men Hear the Good News (Acts 18:24 – 19:6)

Not only did Paul routinely preach in the local synagogues, so did other devout men of faith. One such orator was Apollos, an eloquent scholar who spoke fervently at Ephesus. Although he had only been baptized for repentance according to John the Baptist's doctrine, he spoke with power and wisdom. Aquila and Priscilla took him aside and explained that Jesus had come to save mankind, had been raised from the dead, and gave new life to all who called upon him. Apollos then received Christ and became a convincing evangelist to the Jews.

Following this, Paul found twelve more men in Ephesus who had only been baptized with John's baptism for repentance for sin. So Paul baptized them in water in the name of the Lord Jesus. Next, he laid his hands upon them and "the Holy Ghost came on them; and they spoke with tongues, and prophesied" (Acts 19:6, KJV).

Power over Sickness and Demons (Acts 19:8-20)

Despite opposition, Paul continued to preach powerfully in Ephesus, with signs and wonders following. When his handkerchiefs and aprons were brought to people in need, the sick were healed and the demon-possessed were set free.

On one occasion, God even used counterfeit preachers to illustrate His power. When a few sorcerers, posing as Christians, attempted to cast out a devil, the evil spirit attacked them and wounded them, proving that Paul was a true child of God with power over demons. Every Jew and Greek in Ephesus heard about this and many became Christians. Additionally, many who had been involved in the occult burned their books in a great fire.

Paul's Preaching Bad for Business (Acts 19:23-41)

At the guidance of the Holy Spirit, Paul was planning to leave Ephesus when the city's silversmiths created a great dissension. These tradesmen, who made their livings by producing shrines of the idol Diana, were irate about Paul's preaching because many of their customers were abandoning idol worship. In Paul's absence, the mob dragged a couple of his friends into the vast crowd of rioters, most of whom had no idea of why they were there. The uproar subsided when the arena manager disbursed the crowd by reminding them that no crime had been committed and that no proper trial had been held.

Paul, Timothy and Companions from the Churches (Acts 19:24 – 20:5)

Following the great uproar in Ephesus, Paul set out for Greece, preaching to churches on the way. Following a three month stay in Greece, he planned to sail to Syria, but changed his plans to avoid being killed in another scheme.

So Paul traveled to Macedonia along with several devout believers, including Timothy of Lystra. Paul had recruited traveling companions who were strong in the faith and able ministers. Some of these men came from towns where Paul had preached.

After observing Passover ceremonies in Greece, Paul sailed five days to Turkey, where he stayed a week. There, one of Paul's sermons lasted late into the night and a man fell to his death from the third floor. Paul took the dead man in his arms and declared that he was all right – and the man returned to life! The congregation was ecstatic at this miracle and Paul preached until the sun came up.

Paul Desires to Go to Jerusalem (Acts 21:15 – Acts 26:32)

Despite personal danger, Paul had a strong desire to go to Jerusalem for the celebration of Pentecost. Along his voyage, Paul's vessel stopped in Ephesus and met the church elders at the waterside. Knowing that he would never see these dear friends again, Paul comforted them concerning the suffering he would face in Jerusalem, which had been prophesied to him on several occasions. "But my life is worth nothing to me unless I use it for finishing the work assigned me by the Lord Jesus—the work of telling others the Good News about the wonderful grace of God." (Acts 20:24, TLB). This one statement characterizes Paul's fixation on doing the Lord's work. Finally, Paul challenged the elders of Ephesus to take care of the flock, soberly warning them that the Holy Spirit would hold them responsible.

In Jerusalem, Paul continued to testify. He encouraged church leaders, who were sorrowful about Paul's impending trial. Furthermore, he survived a murderous mob and then had the opportunity to testify to them. But God's constant guidance assured Paul of completing his assignment. "Be of good cheer, Paul: for as you have testified of me in Jerusalem, so must you bear witness also at Rome" (Acts 23:11). Next, a heavily armed Roman contingent escorted Paul to Caesarea, thwarting a plan by 40 zealots to murder him.

From Caesarea to Rome (Acts 24-28)

In Caesarea, the Sadducees and Pharisees, hoping to obtain the death penalty for Paul, vehemently accused him of crimes against the Roman government and of defiling the temple. When the governor could find nothing worthy of death in Paul, he consulted with King Agrippa, who asked to hear Paul himself. This gave Paul another opportunity to fulfill his original commission from the Lord: "to bear my name before the Gentiles, and kings, and the children of Israel (Acts 9:14)."

Paul was then sent by ship to stand trial in Rome. Along the way, Paul was allowed to visit friends in Sidon, but later in the journey, the sailing vessel ran into an extremely violent storm. Yet, God's guidance was ever present when an angel reassured him that he "must be brought before Caesar" (Acts 27:24). After a full two weeks of stormy weather, the ship ran aground and all 276 prisoners and crew escaped to land. There, Paul gained notoriety among the islanders when he survived a deadly snake bite. He also prayed for the healing of the governor's father, who then recovered from fever and dysentery. This news brought droves of sick islanders to Paul, who prayed for them and healed them by God's power.

Eventually, Paul reached Rome where he was allowed to minister, preach, and teach freely. Although he was under guard, these two years were fruitful times of ministry for Paul. Ultimately Paul died as he had lived; in faithful testimony to Christ.

The Evangelized Evangelize

Paul's letters to the various churches he started reveal that they had grown into evangelistic powerhouses themselves. In writing to the Church at Thessalonica, Paul expressed his sincere admiration for their outreach: "Then you yourselves became an example to all the other Christians in Greece. And now *the Word of the Lord has spread out from you to others everywhere*, far beyond your boundaries"

(1 Thessalonians 1:8, TLB). The early evangelists multiplied their efforts through the voices of their converts.

Not only were they willing to proclaim the gospel to others, they were willing to bear hardship and suffering as well. Writing from a prison cell to the pastors, deacons, and other Christians in Philippi, Paul stated: "And because of my imprisonment many of the Christians here seem to have lost their fear of chains! Somehow my patience has encouraged them and they have become more and *more bold in telling others about Christ*" (Philippians 1:14, TLB). Paul's boldness was contagious!

Paul also wrote the following compliment to the church in Rome: "Let me say first of all that wherever I go I hear you being talked about! *For your faith in God is becoming known around the world*" (1 Thessalonians 1:8, TLB). The world could no longer escape the truth of salvation.

The early church never viewed a select few missionaries as the only evangelists qualified to preach the gospel. Every Christian assumed responsibility for telling others about the Lord. This small group of zealous saints, enthralled in the great and thrilling work of evangelism, grew into a worldwide body of every race and nationality. To this very day, each spiritual generation embraces the same gospel proclaimed in the first century.

CONCLUSION

The Great Contribution of the Early Church: *Attitude* (2 Corinthians 11: 25-28)

Attitude is the great contribution of the early church. When put on trial, they testified boldly. When hounded out of town, they preached elsewhere. When jailed, they sang. When beaten, they rejoiced at the privilege of suffering for the Lord. When condemned, they glorified God in their deaths. Each and every attack provided an opportunity to honor the Lord.

Peter was threatened, beaten, jailed, and finally crucified upside down. Paul was beaten with rods three times, stoned once, shipwrecked three times, and left in the ocean overnight. He was hunted, jailed, tried, and insulted. Stephen and James were murdered, as were all of the apostles except John.

Yet they followed wherever the Holy Spirit led. They rejoiced in their mistreatment as "*partakers of Christ's sufferings*" and as those who would one day be rewarded for their sacrifices (1 Peter 4:13, KJV).

In all of this, Peter was able to write: "Dear friends, don't be bewildered or surprised when you go through the fiery trials ahead, for this is no strange, unusual thing that is going to happen to you. Instead, be really glad–because these trials will make you partners with Christ in his suffering, and afterwards you will have the wonderful joy of sharing his glory in that coming day when it will be displayed. ... it is no shame to suffer for being a Christian. Praise

God for the privilege of being in Christ's family and being called by his wonderful name!" (1 Peter 4: 12-14, 16 TLB).

And, although their bodies were here on earth, their hearts were in heaven.

"But now they desire a better country, that is, a heavenly: wherefore God is not ashamed to be called their God: for he has prepared for them a city" (Hebrews 11:16, KJV).

The Future of the Church

Isaiah prophesied that the Lord's reign would *increase* forever. Church growth is a certainty. The work of the early church was only the beginning.

"For unto us a child is born, unto us a son is given: and the government shall be upon his shoulder: and his name shall be called Wonderful, Counselor, The mighty God, the everlasting Father, The Prince of Peace. ***Of the increase of his government and peace there shall be no end***, upon the throne of David, and upon his kingdom, to order it, and to establish it with judgment and with justice from henceforth even forever. The zeal of the Lord of hosts will perform this" (Isaiah 9: 6-7, KJV).

An Example to Follow

The Lord Jesus Christ himself bore the insults, abuse, and hatred of an evil world. He was able to do this by focusing on the reward ahead of him. The apostles and early church members also lived their lives with both eyes on heaven. As Jesus died for the apostles, the apostles died for Christ. They were fixed on eternity and this world had nothing to compare with heaven. They never collapsed, they never gave up, they never changed their minds, and they never regretted a single day in the service of Christ.

The Early Church

A Study in Supernatural Power

QUESTIONS TO CONSIDER

The early church relied upon God's supernatural intervention to evangelize.

> Do you believe in supernatural power?
> Have you ever seen a miracle?
> Do you believe in angels? Why?

Why was there such severe resistance to the gospel?

> By religious authorities?
> By government authorities?
> By business people?
> By the academic community?

Although Paul was quite well known in his day and even to this day, the lesser known Barnabas was a key figure in the early church?

> Does fame always accompany great work?
> Barnabas was less known than Paul. Was he less essential than Paul?

The apostles and the elders in Jerusalem published church doctrine.

What is doctrine?
Why did the apostles and elders inform other churches of accepted doctrine?

Why did the apostles view suffering for Christ as an honor? "And they departed from the presence of the council, rejoicing that they were counted worthy to suffer shame for his name" (Acts 5:41).

How did these early Christians endure suffering?

If you believe in divine providence, you believe things happen "for" us, not "to" us. Is this hard to accept?

"And we know that all things work together for good to them that love God." (Romans 8:28).

Is it possible to know exactly how God will use your experience in the future?

For example, you may have had a bad experience in a previous situation.

Do you know how God will use this to your advantage in the future?

The Early Church

A Study in Supernatural Power

DISCUSSION QUESTIONS AND ACTIVITIES

Discussion: Strangers in Their Own Land

In the face of tremendous persecution, the early church must have felt out of place.

Are you willing to be counted among the persecuted?

How can we make others feel accepted?

Objective: To facilitate new friendships.

Class Discussion: Attitude Determines Your Altitude

The early church went through a great deal of hardship, yet they had a positive attitude.

Proverbs 15:15 says, "But he that is of a merry heart *has* a continual feast."

What attitude is best for your current situation?

What challenges do you face in keeping a good attitude?

Is success harder to handle than failure?

Objective: To consider our response to success and failure.

Discussion: Everybody Cannot Be a Rock Star

Some jobs are less glamorous than others. Does that make them less important?

Objective: To appreciate the contributions of each person, regardless of how visible or noticed the role is.

CHAPTER 11

SCRIPTURES FOR TEAM LEADERS

A group is simply a gathering of people. A team, however, is a gathering of people working together toward a common goal. Each and every member contributes something of value to the effort. The following Bible passages offer enlightenment concerning teams.

Teams have the power to impact the world.

> And when they found them not, they drew Jason and certain brethren unto the rulers of the city, crying, "These **that have turned the world upside down** are come hither also." (Acts 17:6, KJV)

> "Look! If they are able to accomplish all this when they have just *begun* to exploit their linguistic and political unity, just think of what they will do later! Nothing will be unattainable for them! (Genesis 11:6, TLB)

So built we the wall; and all the wall was joined together unto the half thereof: for the people had a mind to work. (Nehemiah 4:6, KJV)

For if they fall, the one will lift up his fellow: but woe to him that is alone when he falls; for he has not another to help him up. (Ecclesiastes 4:10)

This job is too heavy a burden for you to handle all by yourself. Find some **capable, honest** men. They will help you carry the load, making the task easier for you. Then you will be able to endure the pressures. (Exodus 18:18A, 21A, 22B, 23B, The Book, NLT)

Teams Experience Challenges

JEALOUSY

And when the ten heard it, they were moved with indignation against the two brethren. (Matthew 20:24, KJV)

There was also rivalry among them concerning which of them was to be counted the greatest.. (Luke 22:24, MEV)

TEAMS LOSE MEMBERS

- John the Baptist was beheaded.
- Jonathan, David's closest ally, was killed in battle.
- Uriah the Hittite was murdered by his own commander.
- God took Moses home before the Jews entered the Promised Land.

THE WHOLE TEAM MAY SUFFER BECAUSE OF ONE PERSON'S MISTAKES

When I saw among the plundered goods a beautiful robe from Babylon, two hundred shekels of silver, and a gold bar weighing fifty shekels, I coveted them, so I took them. They are hidden in the ground in my tent. The silver is underneath them." Then Joshua said, "Why have you brought trouble on us? The LORD will trouble you today!" (Joshua 7:21 and 25, MEV)

SOME TEAM MEMBERS MAY CATCH ON SLOWLY AND FRUSTRATE THE LEADERS.

How could you even think I was talking about food? But again I say, "Beware of the yeast of the Pharisees and Sadducees." (Matthew 16:11, MEV)

Your eyes are to see with—why don't you look? Why don't you open your ears and listen?' Don't you remember anything at all? (Mark 8:18, TLB)

And the people murmured against Moses, saying, What shall we drink? (Exodus 15:24, KJV)

And Miriam and Aaron spoke against Moses.... (Numbers 12:1, KJV)

And they said unto Moses, Because there were no graves in Egypt, have you taken us away to die in the wilderness? (Exodus 14:11, KJV)

SOME TEAM MEMBERS MAY BE MORE INTERESTED IN OTHERS' ROLES THAN IN THEIR OWN

When Peter saw him, he said to Jesus, "Lord, what about this man?" Jesus said to him, "If it is My will that he remains until I come, what is that to you? Follow Me!" (John 21: 21-23, MEV)

He that tills his land shall be satisfied with bread: but he that follows vain persons is void of understanding. (Proverbs 12:11, KJV)

SOME TEAM MEMBERS ARE AFRAID TO TAKE ACTION

I was afraid I would lose your money, so I hid it in the earth. Look, here is your money back. (Matthew 25:25, NLT)

SOME WHO ARE SUPPOSED TO SET THE EXAMPLE ABANDON THE MISSION

Simon Peter said, "I'm going fishing." (John 21:2-3, KJV)

The first time I was brought before the judge, no one came with me. Everyone abandoned me. (2 Timothy 4:16, TLB)

He was one of the three men who, with David, held back the Philistines that time when the rest of the Israeli army fled. He killed the Philistines until his hand was too tired to hold his sword; and the Lord gave him a great victory. (The rest of the army did not return until it was time to collect the loot!) (2 Samuel 23:9,10, TLB)

SOMETIMES TEAM MEMBERS ATTACK THEIR TEAMMATES

I am afraid that I will find you quarreling, and envying each other, and being angry with each other, and acting big, and saying wicked things about each other and whispering behind each other's backs, filled with conceit and disunity. (2 Corinthians 12:20, TLB)

CHARACTERISTICS OF HIGH-PERFORMING TEAMS

ACKNOWLEDGE THE LORD IN THEIR WORK

Abide in me, and I in you. As the branch cannot bear fruit of itself, except it abide in the vine; **no more can you, except you abide in me.** I am the vine, you are the branches: He that abides in me, and I in him, the same brings forth much fruit: for without me you can do nothing. (Jesus, in John 15: 4-5, KJV)

Trust in the Lord with all your heart; and lean not unto thine own understanding.

In all your ways **acknowledge him**, and he shall direct your paths. (Proverbs 3: 5-6, KJV)

Unless the LORD builds the house, the builders labor in vain. Unless the LORD watches over the city, the guards stand watch in vain. (Psalms 127:1, NIV)

ARE UNITED

Now I beseech you, brethren, by the name of our Lord Jesus Christ, that you all speak the same thing, and that there be no divisions among you; but that you are perfectly joined together in **the same mind** and in the same judgment. (1 Corinthians 1:10, KJV)

Can two walk together, except they are agreed? (Amos 3:3, KJV)

HAVE A VISION

And the LORD answered me, and said, Write the vision, and make it plain upon tables, that he may run that reads it. (Habakkuk 2:2, KJV)

RECRUIT TALENTED PEOPLE

Then the LORD said to Moses, "Look, I have specifically chosen Bezalel son of Uri, grandson of Hur, of the tribe of Judah. I have filled him with the Spirit of God, giving him great wisdom, ability, and expertise in all kinds of crafts. He is a master craftsman, expert in working with gold, silver, and bronze. He is skilled in engraving and mounting gemstones and in carving wood. He is a master at every craft! (Exodus 31:1-5, NLT)

Them has he filled with wisdom of heart, to work all manner of work. (Exodus 35:35, KJV)

FIND PEOPLE WHO ARE NATURAL TEAM PLAYERS

For I have no man likeminded, who will naturally care for your state.

ARE FOCUSED

I therefore so run, not as uncertainly; so fight I, not as one that beats the air (1 Corinthians 9:26, KJV)

No man that wars entangles himself with the affairs of this life; that he may please him who has chosen him to be a soldier. (2 Timothy 2:4, KJV)

COUNT THE COSTS

Or what king, going to make war against another king, sits not down first, and consults whether he be able with ten thousand to meet him that comes against him with twenty thousand? (Luke 14:31, KJV)

Send men, that they may search the land of Canaan ... (Numbers 13:2, KJV)

COMMUNICATE FRANKLY WITH ONE ANOTHER

Then I said to them, "You see the bad situation we are in." (Nehemiah 2:17, KJV)

Open rebuke is better than secret love. (Proverbs 27:5, KJV)

ARE ACCOUNTABLE for THEIR ACTIONS

Moreover, it is required in stewards (team members), that a man be found faithful. (1 Corinthians 4:2, KJV)

GET CONTRIBUTIONS FROM EVERY MEMBER OF THE TEAM

If the whole body were an eye, where were the hearing? If the whole were hearing, where were the smelling? (1 Corinthians 12:17, KJV)

No, those parts of the body that seem to be weaker are actually very important. (1 Corinthians 12:22, TLB)

Just as there are many parts to our bodies, so it is with Christ's body. We are all parts of it, and it takes every one of us to make it complete, for we each have different work to do. So we belong to each other, and each needs all the others. (Romans 12:4, TLB)

CARE FOR EACH OTHER AND TAKE CARE OF EACH OTHER

The parts have the same care for each other that they do for themselves. If one part suffers, all parts suffer with it, and if one part is honored, all the parts are glad. (1 Corinthians 12: 25, 26 TLB)

Don't be selfish; don't live to make a good impression on others. Be humble, thinking of others as better than yourself. Don't just think about your own affairs, but be interested in others, too, and in what they are doing. Your attitude should be the kind that was shown us by Jesus Christ, who, though he was God, did not demand and cling to his rights as God, but laid aside his mighty power and glory, taking the disguise of a slave and becoming like men. And he humbled himself even further, going so far as actually to die a criminal's death on a cross. (Philippians 2: 3-8, TLB)

Bear one another's burdens, and so fulfil the law of Christ. (Galatians 6:2, KJV)

But if the watchman sees the enemy coming and doesn't sound the alarm and warn the people, he is responsible for their deaths. They will die in their sins, but I will charge the watchman with their deaths. (Ezekiel 33:6, TLB)

We give thanks to God always for you all, making mention of you in our prayers;

Remembering without ceasing your work of faith, and labor of love, and patience of hope in our Lord Jesus Christ, in the sight of God and our Father. (1 Thessalonians 1: 2, 3, KJV)

Rejoice with them that do rejoice, and weep with them that weep. (Romans 12:15, KJV)

VALUE AND REWARD ALL TEAM MEMBERS

We share and share alike-those who go to battle and those who guard the equipment. (1 Samuel 30:24 TLB)

People who take care of fig trees are allowed to eat the fruit. In the same way, people who take care of their masters will be rewarded. (Proverbs 27:18, ERV)

His lord said unto him, Well done, good and faithful servant: you have been faithful over a few things, I will make you ruler over many things: enter into the joy of your Lord. (Matthew 25:21)

In all the work you are given, do the best you can. Work as though you are working for the Lord, not any earthly master. Remember that you will receive your reward from the Lord, who will give you what he promised his people. Yes, you are serving Christ. He is your real Master. Remember that anyone who does wrong will be punished for that wrong. And the Lord treats everyone the same. (Colossians 3:23-25, ERV)

ADDRESS LEGITIMATE COMPLAINTS OF THE TEAM MEMBERS

More and more people were becoming followers of Jesus. But during this same time, the Greek-speaking followers began to complain about the Jewish followers. They said that their widows were not getting their share of what the followers received every day. The twelve apostles called the whole group of followers together.

The apostles said to them, "It would not be right for us to give up our work of teaching God's word in order to be in charge of getting food to people. So, brothers and sisters, choose seven of your men who have a good reputation. They must be full of wisdom and the Spirit. We will give them this work to do." (Acts 6: 1-3, KJV)

REINFORCE GOOD WORK

Now let me remind you ... (1 Corinthians 15, KJV)

And that these days should be remembered and kept throughout every generation, every family, every province, and every city. (Esther 9:28, KJV)

Wherefore I put you in remembrance that you stir up the gift of God, which is in you. (2 Timothy 1:6, KJV)

And you shall teach them ordinances and laws, and shall show them the way wherein they must walk, and the work that they must do. (Exodus 18:20, KJV)

And you shall write them upon the door posts of your house, and upon your gates. (Deuteronomy 11:20, KJV)

ARE OBEDIENT

Servants, obey in all things your masters according to the flesh; not with eyeservice, as men-pleasers; but in singleness of heart, fearing God: And whatsoever you do, do it **heartily**, as to the Lord, and not unto men; Knowing that of the Lord you shall receive the reward of the inheritance: for you serve the Lord Christ. (Colossians 3: 22-24, KJV)

And Simon answering said unto him, Master, we have toiled all the night, and have taken nothing: **nevertheless, at your word** I will let down the net. (Luke 5:5, KJV)

Christian slaves (employees) should work hard for their owners and respect them; never let it be said that Christ's people are poor workers. Don't let the name of God or his teaching be laughed at because of this. If their owner is a Christian, that is no excuse for slowing down; rather they should **work all the harder because a brother in the faith is being helped by their efforts.** (1 Timothy 6:1-2 TLB)

Work hard so God can say to you, "Well done." (2 Timothy 2:15 TLB)

DON'T VERBALLY ATTACK FELLOW TEAM MEMBERS

Of these things put them in remembrance, charging them before the Lord that they strive not about words to no profit, but to the subverting of the hearers. (2 Timothy 2:14, KJV)

So we, though many, are one body in Christ, and individually members one of another. (Romans 12:5, ESV)

If it be possible, as much as lies in you, live peaceably with all men. (Romans 12:18, KJV)

DO NOT WASTE TIME

Teach us to number our days and recognize how few they are; help us to spend them as we should. (Psalms 90:12 TLB)

If you wait for perfect conditions, you will never get anything done. (Ecclesiastes 11:4, KJV)

Then Joshua asked them, "How long are you going to wait before clearing out the people living in the land which the Lord your God has given to you?" (Joshua 18:3 TLB)

Don't be fools; be wise: **make the most of every opportunity** you have for doing good. (Ephesians 5:16 TLB)

Use your time in the best way you can. (Colossians 4:5, ERV)

INVEST IN TRAINING AND EDUCATION

Wise people want to learn more, so they listen closely to gain knowledge. (Proverbs 18:15, ERV)

A dull axe requires great strength; be wise and sharpen the blade. (Ecclesiastes 10:10)

The more you learn, the more you earn.
The more you know, the more you grow.

DON'T RUSH TO JUDGEMENT ABOUT OTHER TEAM MEMBERS

Jesus told this story: "A man had a fig tree. He planted it in his garden. He came looking for some fruit on it, but he found none. He had a servant who took care of his garden. So, he said to his servant, 'I have been looking for fruit on this tree for three years, but I never find any. Cut it down! Why should it waste the ground?' But the servant answered, 'Master, let the tree have one more year to produce fruit. Let me dig up the dirt around it and fertilize it. Maybe the tree will have fruit on it next year. If it still does not produce, then you can cut it down.'" (Luke 13:6-9, ERV)

I beseech you for my son Onesimus, whom I have begotten in my bonds: which in time past was to you unprofitable, but now profitable to you and to me: (Philemon 1: 10-11, KJV)

Judge not according to the appearance, but **judge righteous judgment**. (John 7:24, KJV)

Wise people think before they act, fools don't. (Proverbs 13:16 NLT)

… for the Lord sees not as man sees; for man looks on the outward appearance, but **the Lord looks on the heart**. (1 Samuel 16:7, KJV)

STICK WITH IT UNTIL THE JOB IS DONE

Better is the end of a thing than the beginning thereof: and the patient in spirit is better than the proud in spirit. (Ecclesiastes 7:8, KJV)

And let us not be weary in well doing: for in due season we shall reap, if we faint not. (Galatians 6:9, KJV)

But you, brethren, be not weary in well doing. (2 Thessalonians 3:13, KJV)

SEIZE THE OPPORTUNITY TO WORK

Ants have no ruler, no boss, and no leader. But in the summer, ants gather all of their food and save it. So when winter comes, there is plenty to eat. (Proverbs 6:7-9, ERV)

EXPECT and PREPARE FOR SUCCESS

The Lord says to fill this dry valley with trenches to hold the water he will send. (2 Kings 3:16, TLB)

Get ready to cross the Jordan River. "In three days, we will go across and conquer. and live in the land which God has given us!" he told them. (Joshua 1:10 TLB)

SEEK HELP FROM GOD

Let the Lord our God favor us and give us success.

May he give permanence to all we do. (Psalms 90:17, KJV)

CHAPTER 12

The True Team Leader

For guaranteed success, you _must_ have one team leader: God.

2 Corinthians 2:14. But I thank God, who always leads us in victory because of Christ.

John 15:4. Take care to live in me, and let me live in you. For a branch can't produce fruit when severed from the vine. Nor can you be fruitful apart from me.

Your team's success depends on God.

1 Corinthians 3:6 NLT.
I planted the seed in your hearts, and Apollos watered it, but it was God who made it grow.

You are on God's team.
We are workers together for God. (1 Corinthians 3:6, ERV)

Don't be timid about asking God for help:
You have not, because you ask not. (James 4:2)

Matthew 18:20.
For where two or three are gathered together **in my name**, there am I in the midst of them.

ASK THE LORD TO JOIN AND LEAD YOUR TEAM

John 6:20,21.
But he said unto them, "It is I; be not afraid."
Then they willingly received him into the ship: and **immediately the ship was at the land** whither they went.

Your Team's Success Depends on Obedience to God.

David, in 2 Samuel 22:22-25

For I have kept the ways of the Lord, and have not wickedly departed from my God. For all his judgments were before me: and as for his statutes, I did not depart from them. I was also upright before him, and have kept myself from my iniquity. **Therefore, the Lord has recompensed me according to my righteousness; according to my cleanness in his eye sight.**

Leviticus 26:1-4, ERV.

"Don't make idols for yourselves. Don't set up statues or memorial stones in your land to bow down to, because I am the LORD your God!

"Remember my special days of rest and honor my holy place. I am the LORD.

"Remember my laws and commands, and obey them. If you do these things, I will give you rains at the time they should come. The land will grow crops and the trees of the field will grow their fruit."

Proverbs 16:7.

When a man's ways please the Lord, he makes even his enemies to be at peace with him.

Psalms 127:1-2, TLB.

Unless the Lord builds a house, the builders' work is useless. Unless the Lord protects a city, sentries do no good. It is senseless for you to work so hard from early morning until late at night, fearing you will starve to death; for God wants his loved ones to get their proper rest.

But, you need to be aware that ...

It is a *fearful thing* to fall into the hands of the living God.
Hebrews 10:31

God destroys <u>anything</u> that comes between Him and you.
If you depart from God, He will scatter your team.

Psalm 73:27
For, lo, they that are far from you shall perish: you have destroyed all them that go a whoring from you.

Leviticus 26:14-26, ERV

"But if you don't obey me and all my commands, bad things will happen to you. If you refuse to obey my laws and commands, you have broken my agreement. If you do that, I will cause terrible things to happen to you. I will cause you to have disease and fever. They will destroy your eyes and take away your life. You will not have success when you plant your seed. And your enemies will eat your crops. For, lo, they that are far from you shall perish: you have destroyed all them that go a whoring from you. (Psalms 73:27)

Work hard and cheerfully at all you do, just as though you were working for the Lord and not merely for your masters, remembering that it is the Lord Christ who is going to pay you, giving you your full portion of all he owns. He is the one you are really working for. ***And if you don't do your best for him, he will pay you in a way that you won't like.*** (Paul, in Colossians 3:23-25, *The Living Bible*)

Deuteronomy 32: 29-30 The Living Bible

Oh, that they were wise! Oh, that they could understand!

Oh, that they would know what they are getting into!

How could one single enemy chase a thousand of them,

And two put ten thousand to flight,

Unless their Rock had abandoned them,

Unless the Lord had destroyed them?

CPSIA information can be obtained
at www.ICGtesting.com
Printed in the USA
BVHW090935141220
595665BV00010B/297